Junior Certificate

Science Revision Handbook

Brian Smyth

THE EDUCATIONAL COMPANY

First published 1996
The Educational Company of Ireland
Ballymount Road
Walkinstown
Dublin 12

A trading unit of Smurfit Services Ltd.

Design And Layout: Phototype-Set
Artwork: Daghda
Cover design: Design Image
Printed in the Republic of Ireland by Smurfit Web Press

0 1 2 3 4 5 6 7 8 9   (ASC 8011S)

The paper used in this book comes from Managed Forests in Northern Europe For every tree felled, at least one new tree is planted

Preface

This book is intended as a revision aid for students about to sit their Junior Certificate in Science. It provides concise key points for each section of the course and a comprehensive set of questions on each topic. All four sections of the course are covered. The questions are designed to bring the student through the entire science syllabus and they are similar to the type of question that the student will encounter in the Junior Certificate examination. The concise nature of the key points will enable the student to revise the entire course in the days leading up the examination. Each chapter is split up into small manageable sections to facilitate revision.

I would like to acknowledge and thank the staff of the Educational Company for their work on this book, to Frank Fahy, Chief Editor, for initiating the project, to Robert McLoughlin for his interest in the project, to the artist who transformed my crude drawings to presentable diagrams and to Anthony Murray and Aengus Carroll, a special thanks for their patience, perseverance and encouragement throughout the entire project.

Brian Smyth

Ⓗ For Higher Level only

Physics

Chemistry

Biology

Applied Science

Chapter 1   PHYSICS

Introduction

Key Points

1. **Matter** is anything which has mass or which occupies space. Matter exists in **three states**, **solid**, **liquid** and **gas**.

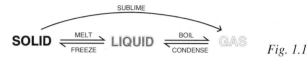

Fig. 1.1

2. To measure length use:
   a. a metre stick
   b. a tape measure
   c. a vernier callipers
   d. an opisometer
   e. a trundle wheel
   Unit: **metre**, **centimetre**.

3. The **volume** of a body is how much space it takes up. Units, m^3, cm^3. The volume of a liquid can be measured using a graduated cylinder and the volume of a small solid can be found using an overflow can in conjunction with a graduated cylinder.
   Fig. 1.2

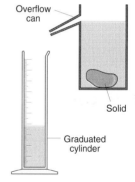

Fig. 1.2

4. The **mass** of a body is the quantity of matter in it. Mass is measured by a weighing scales.
   Unit: **gram (g)**, **kilogram (kg)**.

5. **Time** is measured by a clock or a watch or a stopwatch.
   Unit: **second (s)**.

Questions

1. What is matter? Name the three states of matter.

2. What is sublimation?

3. On what does the state of matter depend?

4. What is meant by:
   (i)   the melting point of a solid,
   (ii) the boiling point of a liquid?

5. How would you measure:
   (i)   The length of a river on a map.
   (ii)   The inside and outside diameter of a small pipe.
   (iii) The length of a rugby pitch.
   (iv)   The length of a desk.
   (v)   The length of a pencil.

6. How would you find the volume of:
   (i)   a pebble
   (ii)   a regular piece of timber
   (iii) a quantity of liquid ($< 100cm^3$)

7. How would you measure the mass of:
   (i)   a marble
   (ii)   a piece of timber
   (iii) the tea in a cup
   (iv)   a sheet of paper
   (v)   a pin

8. How would you measure the time it takes to run 100m?

Energy

Key Points

1. **Energy is the ability to do work.** Energy has the ability to move things, e.g. heat, light, sound and electricity are all forms of energy.

2. **Kinetic energy is the energy a body has when it moves**, e.g. a car driving along a motorway, a hand moving around a clock face.

3. **Potential energy is stored energy or the energy that a body has due to its position**, e.g. a boulder on top of a hill has potential energy. When it starts to roll down the hill the potential energy is converted to kinetic energy. A clock spring, a battery, a lump of coal, a loaf of bread all have potential energy.

4. **Law of Conservation of Energy**: Energy cannot be created or destroyed but it may be converted from one form to another. See Energy Conversion on page 106.

5. There are many ways of heating a house – gas, oil, coal, turf, electricity.

6. An **insulator** prevents heat loss and therefore increases the efficiency of a heating system, e.g. attic insulation, double glazing, a lagging jacket on the hot water cistern.

7. **Non-renewable energy sources** are sources of energy that will eventually run out. They include coal, oil, turf and natural gas.

8. **Renewable energy sources** can be used over and over again. They will not run out. They include biomass, solar power, wave energy, wind energy, hydroelectric power. It is possible to harness these to generate electricity.

9. Some large atoms such as uranium can split (*Fig. 1.3*) (**nuclear fission**) releasing huge quantities of energy. When the energy is uncontrolled we have a nuclear weapon but when the energy is controlled it can be harnessed to produce electricity. Radioactive substances may also be used to preserve food and they are used in medicine as tracers and in the treatment of cancers.

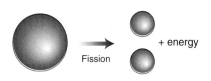

Fig. 1.3

10. **Nuclear fusion** occurs when two light nuclei come together and release energy (*Fig. 1.4*). This reaction occurs in the sun where two atoms of hydrogen combine to produce helium. Nuclear fusion reactions have not yet been developed by scientists, but it does promise a clean, abundant supply of energy.

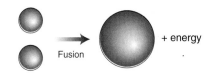

Fig. 1.4

Questions

1. What is energy? List four forms of energy.

2. State the law of conservation of energy. Give two examples of the conversion of one form of energy to another.

3. Define kinetic energy. Give three examples of a body which has kinetic energy.

4. Define potential energy. Give three examples of potential energy.

5. What is an insulator? List five methods of insulating a house against heat loss.

6. What is the difference between renewable and non-renewable sources of energy? Give three examples of each type of energy.

7. There are many forms of renewable energy. Which types could be successfully developed in Ireland? Give reasons for your answer.

8. Consider the fossil fuels listed: coal, oil, turf, gas.
   (a) Which is the easiest to obtain?
   (b) Which is the cheapest to extract?
   (c) What are the dangers associated with
       (i) coal mining
       (ii) extracting oil
       (iii) obtaining gas?
   (d) Which fossil fuel poses the greatest threat to the environment?
       How has this problem been tackled in Ireland?

9. Distinguish between nuclear fusion and nuclear fission.

10. You read in a newspaper that it is proposed to build a nuclear power station in your area. Would you agree with this proposal? Give two advantages and two disadvantages of such a project.

11. Besides nuclear power, give three other uses of radioactive substances.

12. Describe an experiment to show that the rate of heat loss can be reduced by insulation.

13. A man spent £600 on heating bills for a year. He then got his house insulated and found that his heating bill was reduced by 40%. How much did he save in the first year?

Mass, Density, Motion

Key Points

1. The **mass** of a body is the quantity of matter in it.
   Unit: **kilogram (kg)**.

2. **Matter** is anything that has mass and occupies space.

3. **Density** is mass per unit volume. Density = mass/volume. It is measured in g/cm^3.

4. If the density of an object is less than a liquid the object will float on the liquid.

H 5. **Weight** is the force that the earth exerts on a body.
   $W = mg$, where $g = 10$ m/s/s = acceleration due to gravity, W = weight and m = mass.

6. **Speed = distance/time**.
   Unit: **metres/second**.

H 7. **Velocity = distance/time** in a given direction. Unit: metre/second.

H 8. **Acceleration = velocity/time**, that is the rate of change of velocity with time.
A = $(V_1–V_2)/t$
where A = Accelerator, V_1 = Final Velocity, V_2 = Initial Velocity and t = Time.

Questions

1. What is:
   (a) matter
   (b) mass?

2. What is the density of a substance?

3. How would you find the density of:
   (a) a pebble,
   (b) an irregular piece of wood in the laboratory.
   Draw a diagram of any instrument you use.

H 4. How would you find the density of methylated spirits?

5. Find the density of the following objects:
   (a) A stone that has a mass of 7g and it has a volume of 3.5cm³
   (b) A cork that has a mass of 1.5g and a volume of 10cm³
   (c) A piece of timber that has a mass of 100g and a volume of 110cm³

H 6. Find the density of a liquid, 100g of which occupies 110cm³. Which of the objects in Q.5 will float on this liquid? Explain your answer.

H 7. What is meant by the term "flotation"?

H 8. A ship is made of iron. Iron is more dense that water. Why does the ship float?

9. What is the speed of an object? What unit is speed measured in?

10. A sprinter travels 100 metres in 12 seconds. What is his average speed?

11. A train travels 200km at a speed of 100km/hour. How long does the journey take?

12. A motorist drives at an average of 50km/hour. He sets out at 7.30 a.m. and arrives at his destination at 11.00 a.m. How far did he travel?

H 13. Define velocity. What are the units of velocity?

H 14. What is the difference between speed and velocity?

H 15. Calculate the velocity of a car which travels 200km north in 5 hours.

H 16. Define acceleration. In what units is acceleration measured?

H 17. A car's velocity changes from 5 m/s to 25 m/s in 5 seconds. Find the acceleration of the car.

H 18. A car starts from rest and after 10 seconds it is found that its final velocity is 30 m/s. Calculate the acceleration.

H 19. What is the significance of a negative acceleration?

H 20. The brakes are applied to a train moving at 35 m/s. The train finally comes to rest at the station 70 seconds later. Find the retardation (negative acceleration).

H 21. A cyclist is travelling down a road. The distance travelled and the time taken may be found in the following table.

Time Second	0	1	2	3	4	5	6	7
Distance Metre	1	4	8	12	16	20	24	28

(i)   Graph the results from the table (Time – X axis, Distance – Y axis).
(ii) Use the graph to find the time it takes to cycle:
    (a)   6m
    (b)   26m.
(iii) What distance had the cyclist travelled in:
    (a)   2.5 seconds,
    (b)   4.5 seconds?
(iv) At what speed is the cyclist travelling?
(v)   Is the cyclist accelerating?
(vi) What distance will the cyclist have travelled in 9 seconds?

H 22. A car moves from rest and the velocity and the time are recorded below:

Velocity (m/s)	0	3	6	9	12	15	18	21
Time(s)	0	1	2	3	4	5	6	7

(i)   Graph the results (Time – X axis, Velocity – Y axis).
(ii) Is the velocity constant?
(iii) Is the car accelerating?
(iv) What is the velocity after 3.5 seconds?
(v)   When is the velocity 16 m/s?
(vi) Find the acceleration.
    Is it a retardation? Explain.

H 23. The graph (*Fig. 1.5*) shows distance plotted against time.
   (i)   Is the velocity constant?
   (ii) Is the body accelerating?
       Find the acceleration.
  (iii) What distance is travelled in 3.5 seconds?
  (iv) How long does it take to travel 5m?
   (v) Calculate the velocity.

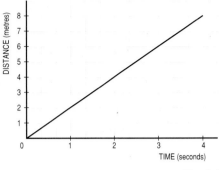

Fig. 1.5

H 24. The graph (*Fig. 1.6*) shows velocity plotted against time.
   (i)   Is the velocity constant?
   (ii) Is the body accelerating?
       Find the acceleration.
  (iii) What is the velocity after 4.5 seconds?
  (iv) How long does it take to reach a velocity of 17 m/s?
   (v) How long does it take to go from 5 m/s to 30 m/s?

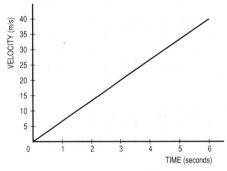

Fig. 1.6

H 25. A car travelling at 35 m/s has the brakes applied and the resulting data was obtained:

Velocity m/s	35	30	25	20	15	10	5	0
Time Second	1	2	4	6	8	10	12	14

   (i)   Graph the results
   (ii) Is the velocity constant?
  (iii) Is the car accelerating?
  (iv) What is the velocity after 7 seconds?
   (v) When is the car travelling at 7.5 m/s?

Forces

Key Points

H 1. A **force is** anything that causes a body to move or to change its velocity in magnitude or direction. The unit of force is the **Newton**. Examples of force include friction, turning, twisting, pulling, pushing, gravity (this is the force of attraction of the earth for an object).

(H) 2. **To every action there is an equal and opposite reaction.**

(H) 3. **Momentum** is the product of the mass of an object by its velocity.
Momentum = mass x velocity.

4. **Friction** is the force of attraction between two surfaces which tries to prevent them from moving. For example, the brakes on an bicycle. Friction is reduced by lubricating the surfaces, e.g. oiling a bicycle chain, greasing bearings.

(H) 5. **Weight** is the force that the earth exerts on a body.
Weight = mass x acceleration due to gravity. W = Mg.

6. A **lever** is any rigid bar or body which is free to rotate about a fixed point called a **fulcrum**.

(H) 7. **The law of the lever states** that when a lever is balanced under any number of forces, the sum of the anti-clockwise moments is equal to the sum of the clockwise moments.
The moment of a force is the product of the force by the distance of that force from the fulcrum**.**

(H) 8. The **centre of gravity of** an object is the point through which the weight of the object appears to act.

(H) 9. A body is in **stable equilibrium** when the fulcrum is above the centre of gravity.
A body is in **neutral equilibrium** when the fulcrum is at the centre of gravity.
A body is in **unstable equilibrium** when the fulcrum is below the centre of gravity.

(H) 10. **Work = force x distance.**
Unit: **Newton metre** or **Joule**.

(H) 11. **Energy is the ability to do work.**

Questions

1. List four effects of a force and give an example of each.

(H) 2. What is a force? Name the unit of force.

(H) 3. 'To every action there is an equal and opposite reaction.' Give three examples to illustrate this statement.

H 4. What do you understand by the term momentum? Why is it more difficult to stop a train travelling at 10 km/hr than a car travelling at the same speed?

H 5. What is the momentum of a 1000 kg car with a velocity of 25 m/s?

H 6. A 1500 kg lorry has a momentum of 30,000 kgm/s. At what speed is the lorry travelling?

H 7. When a bullet is fired from a gun, the gun recoils. Explain in terms of momentum what happens.

8. What is friction? Give two examples of where friction is useful and two examples of where friction is not useful.

H 9. Define work? What is the unit of work?
Calculate the work done when a 50 kg mass is moved 10 metres.
(Note: convert mass to weight. $W = Mg$ where g = acceleration due to gravity).

H 10. If the work done on moving an object 20 metres is 1500 Joules, calculate the
(i)   weight of the object,
(ii) mass of the object.

H 11. A 2 kg shot is thrown a distance X doing 200 J. of work, calculate the distance X.

H 12. What is the centre of gravity of an object?
What is meant by saying that an object is in:
(i)   stable
(ii) neutral
(iii) unstable equilibrium?
Give an example in each case.

H 13. Describe how you would find the centre of gravity of an irregular piece of cardboard.

H 14. If you were designing a sports car, what two features would you incorporate into your design to increase the stability of the car? Give reasons for your answer.

15. What is a lever? Name five levers that you would find around the house.

H 16. State the law of the lever. What is the moment of force? Describe an experiment to demonstrate the law of the lever.

H 17. In the following problems work out the value of D or W as appropriate in each case, so that the lever is balanced.

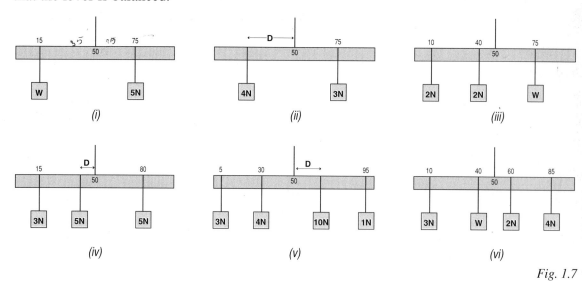

Fig. 1.7

H 18. Which, if any, of the following levers is balanced?

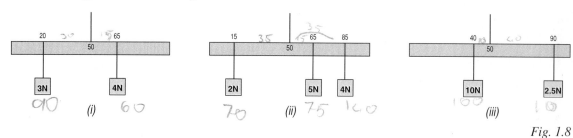

Fig. 1.8

Pressure

Key Points

H 1. **Pressure = Force/Area.** The unit is **N/m²**. This unit is called the **Pascal**.

H 2. When force is distributed over a large area the pressure is small and when pressure is concentrated on a small area the pressure is large. Examples: skis – the ski exerts a small pressure on the snow because the area of the ski is large: a drawing pin – a large pressure can be exerted on the head of a drawing pin, because the area of the drawing pin is small.

H 3. In a **liquid** the pressure is proportional to the density and the depth of the liquid. The pressure in a liquid acts equally in all directions.

H 4. The atmosphere exerts pressure which can be measured with a **barometer**. High pressure gives us dry weather in the summer and dry cold weather in the winter. Low pressure gives us wet and cloudy weather in the summer and wet and mild weather in the winter.

Questions

1. What do understand by the word pressure? How would you design snow shoes so that they will not sink into the snow? How would you design a garden spade so the it will cut into the ground?

H 2. Define pressure. In what units is pressure measured?

H 3. The rectangular block in *Fig 1.9* weighs 200 N. What is the pressure exerted by each of its three sides A, B, C.

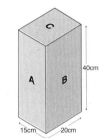
Fig. 1.9

H 4. How would you demonstrate in the lab that the pressure in liquids acts equally in all directions?

H 5. Indicate the water level in vessel A. *(Fig. 1.10)* What would happen if 100cm³ of water was added to the vessel at B?

H 6. Under ideal conditions where should the reservoir for a town be sited? Why? What extra device would you need to install if the reservoir were positioned at a lower level than the town?

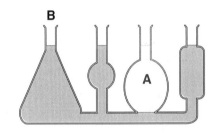
Fig. 1.10

H 7. *Fig. 1.11* shows a drawing pin is being pushed into a piece of timber. What is the pressure at the head and the point of the drawing pin if the force used is 5N?

8. Describe two experiments to show that the atmosphere exerts pressure. Illustrate your answer by diagrams.

H 9. Name three instruments that measure atmospheric pressure.

H 10. Describe how you would construct a mercury barometer in the laboratory. Why do we not actually construct this piece of apparatus now?

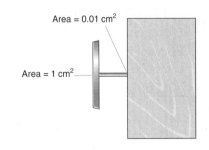
Fig. 1.11

H 11. Mercury and Aneroid barometers both measure atmospheric pressure. Give two advantages of using an Aneroid barometer?

H 12. How does atmospheric pressure vary as we ascend? Name one instrument based on this principle.

H 13. Does the boiling point of liquids rise or fall as we ascend? Give a reason for your answer.

H 14. In what unit do we measure atmospheric pressure?

H 15. What type of weather would you expect in Ireland during the:
(a) summer
(b) winter, under:
(i) high pressure
(ii) low pressure conditions?

H 16. Would it be possible to construct a water barometer? What practical limitations would make it difficult to construct such a device?

Heat

Key Points

1. Heat is a form of **energy**. It is measured in **Joules**. The heat of a body depends on the temperature, mass and the type of material, e.g. the temperature of a cup of water and a swimming pool of water may be the same but the swimming pool has more heat.

2. **Conduction** is the transfer of heat through solids without the substance moving. But the atoms of the solid vibrate.
   Convection is the transfer of heat through a gas or a liquid where the heat is carried by the movement of the particles of the substance.
   Radiation is the movement of heat by electromagnetic rays. It is the way that the sun's heat reaches earth. It does not require a medium to travel.

3. The **temperature** of a body is a measure of how hot the body is. Temperature is measured in degrees Kelvin or degrees Celsius.
   To convert from Kelvin to Celsius subtract 273.
   To convert from Celsius to Kelvin add 273.

	Celsius	Kelvin
Absolute zero	−273°	0°
Melting ice	0°	273°
Body temperature	37°	310°
Boiling water	100°	373°

4. Temperature is measured using a **thermometer**. Two types of thermometer in common usage are an alcohol thermometer and a mercury thermometer.

Mercury thermometer	Alcohol thermometer
less sensitive than alcohol thermometer	more sensitive than mercury thermometer
easy to see	dye needs to be added to see it
range −39° to 350°C	−140°C to 75°C

5. **Black surfaces** radiate and absorb heat more efficiently than shiny surfaces.

6. An **insulator** prevents heat loss by conduction, e.g. clothes, double glazing, vacuum flask. The tog value tells us how good an insulator is a certain material, e.g. a tog value is found on duvets.

7. Solids, liquids and gases expand on heating and contract on cooling.
(H) The **bimetallic strip** consists of two metals bonded together one of which expands more than the other on heating. It therefore bends on heating. It is used in fire alarms and in thermostats.

8. Water expands by approx. 9% of its volume on freezing and so it may damage pipes and car engines when it freezes.

(H) 9. **Latent heat** is the heat absorbed or released when a material changes state without a change in temperature.

(H) 10. Increase in pressure raises the boiling point of a liquid and decrease in pressure lowers the boiling point of a liquid. Increased pressure lowers the melting point of a solid.

(H) 11. **Sublimation** occurs when a solid is heated and it changes directly to a gas without going through the liquid state, e.g. dry ice, iodine, ammonium chloride.

Questions

1. What is heat? In what units is heat measured?

2. What is the temperature of a body? Give an example to show that heat and temperature are not the same.

3. At what temperature:
   (i)   does water boil
   (ii) does water freeze
   (iii) is a healthy human body?

4. What do you understand by the:
   (i) boiling point
   (ii) melting point of a liquid?

5. How is heat transferred through:
   (i)   solids
   (ii) liquids
   (iii) gases
   (iv) outer space?

6. If you were designing a saucepan, what materials would you use for the saucepan and the handle?

7. Convert:
   (i)   0°C
   (ii) 90°C
   (iii) 150°C to Kelvin.

8. Convert:
   (i)   310°K
   (ii) 373°K
   (iii) 500°K to Celsius.

9. On what principle do thermometers work?

10. Give two differences between a standard mercury thermometer and a clinical thermometer.

11. Compare a mercury thermometer and an alcohol thermometer under the headings:
    (i) range
    (ii) sensitivity.

12. Describe experiments to show that:
    (i)   solids
    (ii) liquids and
    (iii) gases expand on heating.

13. How would you demonstrate that water expands on freezing? One disadvantage of this is that the engine in a car may crack in freezing weather. How may a motorist prevent this occurring? Give one other disadvantage and one advantage of the expansion of water when it freezes.

14. Why does a pond freeze from the top down? Give one advantage of this phenomena.

H 15. What is latent heat?
The graph *(Fig. 1.12)* shows ice being heated until water and then steam are produced. What is happening between:
(i) A and B
(ii) B and C
(iii) C and D
(iv) D and E?
Is it worse to be scalded by steam or boiling water? Explain your answer.

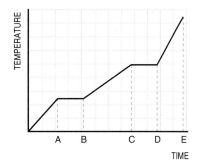

Fig. 1.12

H 16. What is sublimation? Name three materials which sublime.

H 17. Increased pressure lowers the melting point of ice. How would you demonstrate this effect in the laboratory?

H 18. List two advantages of cooking with a pressure cooker. On what principle is the pressure cooker based?

H 19. What is an insulator? Name three methods of insulation found in the home. What does the tog value refer to?

H 20. In *Fig. 1.13* you are given three rods of uniform diameter but of different length. How would you determine which is the best conductor of heat.

Iron

Zinc

Copper

Fig. 1.13

21. Your small sister has sprayed her arm with perfume. She said that it felt cold. Can you explain to her the reason for this?

Electrostatics, Magnetism and Current Electricity

Key Points

A. Electrostatics

H 1. Atoms contain the same number of protons (+ charge) and electrons (– charge), and are therefore electrically neutral. It is sometimes possible to give some substances a charge by either adding or removing electrons, e.g. polythene rubbed with a cloth gains electrons and becomes negatively charged. Perspex rubbed with wool looses electrons and becomes positively charged.

H 2. **Like charges repel** and **unlike charges attract**.

B. Magnetism
1. **Like poles repel** and **unlike poles attract**.

2. A **magnetic field** is the region around a magnet where a magnet exerts influence.

C. Current electricity
1. Electricity is a form of energy and it may be converted to other forms of energy. **Electric current flows from + to –, though the electrons flow from – to +.**

2. **Units.**
   The **Ampere (A)** is the unit of electric current. This can be measured by an ammeter which is placed in series in the circuit.
   The **Volt (V)** is the unit of potential difference. This can be measured by a voltmeter which is placed in parallel in the circuit.
   The **Ohm (Ω)** is the unit of resistance.
   The **Watt (W)** is the unit of power.

3. Relationship between voltage, current, resistance and power.
   Ohms Law: At constant temperature, the current flowing through a resistor is proportional to the potential difference across the resistor.
   $V/I = R$
   The power generated by an appliance is equal to the voltage multiplied by the current
   $W = VI$.

4. The E.S.B. charge by the unit of electricity used. **1 unit = 1 kilowatt hour**. This is the quantity of electricity used when a 1 kilowatt appliance is used for 1 hour. Different electrical appliances have different power ratings and consequently use different quantities of electricity in a given time, e.g. a kilowatt heater uses 1 unit in 1 hour and a 100W bulb uses 1 unit in 10 hours.

5. In an electric circuit a **fuse is fitted as a safety device**. If too high a current flows, the fuse melts and stops the current flowing in the circuit.'

6. Electric current is the flow of electrons through a material. A **conductor** allows electric current to flow and an **insulator** does not allow electric current to flow.
   Electric current flows from a negatively charged body to a positively charged body if they are joined by a conductor.

H

7. Effects of an electric current.

   (a) Heating effect

   To demonstrate this, pass a current through a wire that has a high resistance. The wire heats up. Applications include: electric heater, electric kettle, immersion heater.

   (H) **(b) Chemical effect**

   (i) **Electrolysis of water** is the splitting of water into its elements, hydrogen and oxygen, in a Hoffmann Voltameter, by an electric current.

   (ii) **Electroplating** is covering a metal, e.g. iron, with a second metal, e.g. chromium. It is used to protect one metal or to coat one metal with a more expensive one, e.g. silver plating.

   (H) **(c) Magnetic Effect**

   The magnetic effect of an electric current can be demonstrated using a large current carrying wire and a magnet *(Fig. 1.14)*. The magnetic effect of a solenoid can be demonstrated using a current carrying solenoid and a plotting compass *(Fig. 1.15)*.

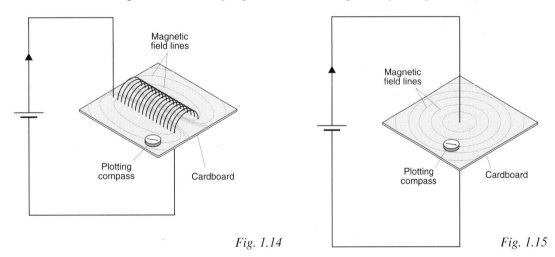

Fig. 1.14   *Fig. 1.15*

8. Domestic Wiring

   The 3 pin plug connects an appliance to the electricity supply.

   (i) **The earth wire** – colour **Yellow/Green**. If a fault develops the current travels to earth and the fuse blows, stopping the flow of current.

   (ii) **The live wire** – colour **brown** – carries the current at 220v. **It also has the fuse.**

   (iii) **The neutral wire** – colour **blue** – is at 0v.

   The sockets and lights are connected in **ring circuits** in the house. A **radial circuit** is used for something like a cooker which uses a lot of power. A **spur** is a method of adding extra sockets, one spur per socket in the ring. The light switch is always connected to the live wire.

   Older houses have a fuse board and more modern houses or houses that have been rewired have **circuit breakers** which switch off the current if it goes above a certain value.

H 9. Resistors in series and parallel are shown in *Fig 1.16*.
For **resistors in series R = R₁ + R₂.**
Calculations are not needed for resistors in parallel.
A variable resistor is called a rheostat and allows
the current to vary in a circuit.

Resistors in series

H 10. **Direct current (D.C.)** always flows in one direction.
Alternating current (A.C.) changes direction many
times a second. In the mains electricity it is 50 cycles
per second. **AC may be changed to DC by means
of a rectifier.**

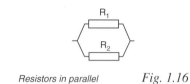

Resistors in parallel   *Fig. 1.16*

Questions

H 1. Explain why atoms are electrically neutral.

H 2. How do some substances such as perspex become charged?

H 3. How would you demonstrate that like charges repel and unlike charges attract?

H 4. What is meant by:
(i)   an electrical insulator
(ii) an electrical conductor.
Give an example of each.

H 5. Conventionally, in which direction does an electric current flow? In which direction do the electrons flow?

6. What is a magnet?

7. How would you show that like magnetic poles repel and unlike magnetic poles attract?

8. What is a magnetic field? How would you show the magnetic field due to a bar magnet in the laboratory? Illustrate your answer with a diagram.

9. Give three uses of magnets.

10. Give three examples to show that electricity is a form of energy.

11. What is an electric current? What are the units of:
(i)   potential difference,
(ii) electric current,
(iii) resistance?

12. What is the relationship between the three quantities in Q.11? What is the relationship called? Describe an experiment to verify this relationship.

13. What instrument is used to measure:
    (i) the voltage across a resistor and
    (ii) the current flowing through a resistor?
    Where are these instruments placed in a circuit?

14. Describe an experiment to show the heating effect on an electric current.

H 15. How would you show the magnetic effect of:
    (i) a current flowing in a long straight wire
    (ii) a current flowing through a solenoid?

H 16. The chemical effect of an electric current is demonstrated by passing current through acidulated water in a Hoffman Voltameter.
    (a) Why is the water acidulated?
    (b) From what element are the electrodes made?
    (c) What reactions occur at the anode and the cathode?
    (e) How would you test these gases to identify them?
    (f) In what ratio do the gases form? What does this tell you about the formula of water?

H 17. In an experiment to plate copper on iron nail:
    (i) At which electrode should the nail be placed?
    (ii) What should the other electrode be made from?
    (iii) Name a suitable electrolyte.
    (iv) List three uses of electroplating.

H 18. In an experiment to prove Ohms Law the following results were obtained

Voltage Volt	2	4	6	8	10	12
Current Amp	0.1	0.2	0.3	0.4	0.5	0.6

    (i) Graph the information in the table. Voltage – Y Axis, Current – X Axis.
    (ii) Does the information prove Ohms Law?
    (iii) Calculate the resistance.
    (iv) What is the voltage at:
        (i) 0.35A,
        (ii) 0.55A?
    (v) What is the current at:
        (i) 3V,
        (ii) 9V?
    (vi) What is a suitable instrument to measure:
        (i) the voltage,
        (ii) the current?
    (vii) Draw a circuit that would give such a set of results.
        What is the relationship between current, voltage and resistance?

H 19. Fill in the gaps in the following table.

Voltage (Volt)	Current (Amp)	Resistance (Ohm)
12	6	?
220	?	11
?	5	6
24	12	?
36	?	3
?	5.5	4

H 20. What is the relationship between power, voltage and current?
Fill the gaps in the following table.

Power (Watt)	Voltage (Volt)	Resistance (Ohm)	Current (Amp)
220	24	?	?
100	?	?	10
?	?	3	4
?	100	20	?
1000	?	?	10
2000	200	?	?

H 21. What is the total resistance of the two resistors in series? The resistors were rearranged in parallel. How would you find their total resistance?
Fig 1.17

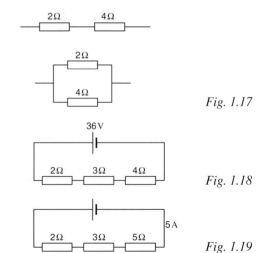

Fig. 1.17

H 22. Find the current flowing in the circuit.
Fig. 1.18

Fig. 1.18

H 23. Find the voltage in the circuit.
Fig. 1.19

Fig. 1.19

24. What unit does the ESB use to charge customers for electricity?

25. How long would it take:
    (a) a 100w bulb
    (b) a 2kw heater
    (c) a 700w hoover
    to use 1 unit of electricity?

26. Calculate the total cost of running the following if electricity costs 8.5p per unit:
    (a) a 150w bulb for 10 hours.
    (b) a 600w hoover for 30 minutes.
    (c) a 2000w heater for 4 hours.

27. How would you conserve electricity in the home?

H 28. What type of current is supplied to the home? What voltage is this usually at?

H 29. If an appliance requires direct current what needs to be done to incoming current?

H 30. How are Christmas tree lights connected? What is a disadvantage of this type of arrangement?

H 31. How are the lights in a house connected? What is the advantage of this type of arrangement?

32. What is the function of:
    (a) a fuse
    (b) the main switch
    (c) a contact breaker?

33. What is a ring circuit? On which wire is the switch placed?

34. What is a spur? How many spurs can be connected to each socket?

35. Name, give the colour code and the function of the three wires that are connected to a three pin plug. Which wire is fused?

36. Why should the correct fuse always be fitted? What would happen if you connected a:
    (i) 10A fuse to an appliance capable of running on 13 amps and
    (ii) a 13A fuse to an appliance which runs on 1 amp?

37. An electric fire is rated at 1kw. What fuse should be fitted if it is connected to a 240 volt supply?

38. What is a short circuit? How are we protected from short circuits in the home?

39. What is the difference between a radial circuit and a ring circuit?

40. What are the advantages of circuit breakers over fuse boards in the modern home?

Light and Sound

Key Points

1. **Light is a form of energy.** It travels at **3×10^8 m/s**.

2. White light is made up of **seven colours**, red, orange, yellow, green, blue, indigo, violet. (Mnemonic: **R**ing **O**ut **Y**our **G**reat **B**ells **I**n **V**ictory)

3. **Dispersion** occurs when white light is broken up into its component colours. This occurs when light is passed through a prism or a diffraction grating.

4. Light can be **reflected** from a surface.

5. Light travels in **straight lines**.

6. A **solar eclipse** happens during the day and it occurs when the moon comes between the sun and the earth, and blocks the light getting to the earth. See page 82.

7. A **lunar eclipse** happens at night and occurs when the earth comes between the sun and the moon. See page 82.

8. Red, green and blue are called the **primary colours**.
   Yellow, cyan and magenta are called the **secondary colours**.
   Two colours, when mixed together to give white light are called **complementary colours**.
   Fig. 1.20

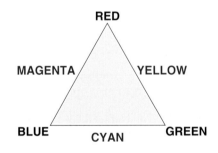

Fig. 1.20

(Mnemonic: **R**emember **Y**our **G**ood **C**lothes **B**efore **M**ass)

Red light + green light + blue light = white light.

A primary colour + its opposite secondary colour = white light
e.g. green light + magenta light = white light.

Two primary colours mixed gives the secondary colour in the middle
e.g. red light + green light = yellow light.

(H) 9. A **wave** is a method of transferring energy through a substance without any overall movement of the substance.
Fig. 1.21

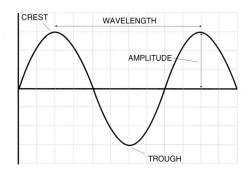

Fig. 1.21

(H) 10. The **frequency** of a wave is the number of crests which pass a point in 1 second. It is measured in Hertz.

(H) 11. The **wavelength** is the distance between two crests.

(H) 12. The **amplitude** is the distance between the centre of the wave and the crest of the wave.

(H) 13. **V = F** λ where
V = the velocity of the wave,
F = the frequency of the wave and
λ = the wavelength.

(H) 14. The **electromagnetic spectrum** consists of:
Gamma rays
X-rays
Ultraviolet rays
Visible light rays
Infra-red rays
Microwaves
Radio waves

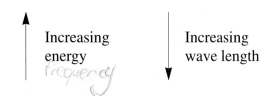

Increasing
energy
frequency

Increasing
wave length

(H) 15. **Refraction** is the bending of light rays when they go from one medium to another, e.g. air to water.
Fig. 1.22

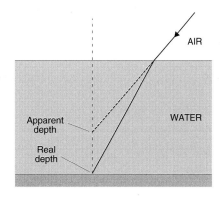

Fig. 1.22

H 16. A **convex lens** causes light to converge and a **concave lens** causes light to diverge.
Fig. 1.23

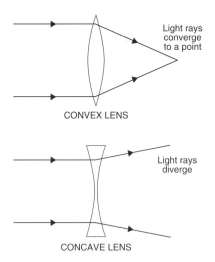

Light rays converge to a point

CONVEX LENS

Light rays diverge

CONCAVE LENS   *Fig. 1.23*

17. **Sound** is a form of energy. It needs a **medium** to travel. The velocity of sound in air is 331 m/s. Reflection of sound is called an **echo**.

18. The **pitch** of the sound depends on the frequency of vibration and the **loudness** depends on the amplitude of the wave.

Questions

1. At what speed does light travel?

2. Give three examples to show that light is a form of energy.

3. What are the seven colours of the rainbow? How would you demonstrate that light is composed of seven colours?
   What is:
   (i)   a primary colour
   (ii) a secondary colour
   (iii) a complementary colour?

   What is meant by the term dispersion of light? Name a piece of apparatus that disperses light. Illustrate your answer with a diagram.

4. What colour light is obtained when the following coloured lights are mixed:
   (a) Red, green and blue
   (b) Red and cyan
   (c) Green and blue
   (d) Magenta and green
   (e) Red and green?

5. Draw a diagram to illustrate:
   (i) a solar eclipse
   (ii) a lunar eclipse.

H 6. What is the:
   (i)   frequency
   (ii) amplitude
   (iii) wavelength of a wave?

H 7. What formula links the velocity, frequency and wavelength of a wave?
Complete the following table.

Velocity m/s	Frequency Hertz	Wavelength m
?	30	300
330	11	?
500	?	25

H 8. From the electromagnetic spectrum, pick the type of wave that:
  (a) gives you a suntan
  (b) heats the earth
  (c) enables us to cook
  (d) helps doctors to cure cancer
  (e) helps doctors to diagnose a broken bone?

For the types of radiation listed above which has the:
  (i) highest frequency
  (ii) the lowest frequency
  (iii) the longest wavelength
  (iv) the shortest wavelength?

9. Describe an experiment to show that light travels in straight lines. Illustrate your answer with a diagram.

10. What do you understand by the reflection of light? A periscope uses reflection of light. Using a diagram describe how a periscope operates.

H 11. What is meant by refraction of light?

H 12. Draw:
  (i) a convex lens
  (ii) a concave lens.

Using a diagram show how you would use these lenses to correct for:
  (i) short sight
  (ii) long sight.

H 13. Identify A, B, C, D in *Fig 1.24*.

14. How would you show that sound needs a medium to carry it?

15. What is an echo? List three uses of echoes.

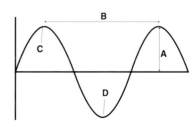

Fig. 1.24

16. What is the speed of:
    (i) sound
    (ii) light?
    Give two examples to show that light travels faster than sound.

H 17. How would you demonstrate that sound is a form of energy?

H 18. How would you demonstrate that sound is a wave motion?

H 19. What is ultrasound?

H 20. On what are the:
    (i) loudness
    (ii) pitch of a note dependent?

21. Give two differences between sound waves and light waves.

22. In the diagram red, green and blue light are shining onto a white screen. What colour light appears in regions A, B, C, D?
    Fig 1.25

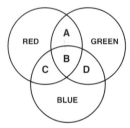

Fig. 1.25

H 23. A man fires a gun. He hears the echo from a cliff 0.6 seconds later. If the speed of sound is 330 m/s, how far away is the cliff?

H 24. A woman hits a golf ball. A second woman standing 170m away hears the club hitting the ball 0.5 seconds later. What is the speed of sound in air?

H 25. Given that the speed of sound in air is 330 m/s. An observer is 100m from a car crash. How long after the crash will he hear the bang?

Chapter 2   CHEMISTRY

Matter, Atoms, Molecules

Key Points

1. **Matter** has **mass** and occupies space. It exists in **three states, solid, liquid** and **gas**.
   The state of matter depends on the degree of movement of the particles which is temperature dependent.

2. **Diffusion** is the movement of particles from a region of high concentration to a region of low concentration.

3. **Brownian motion** is the random zig-zag motion of particles in a liquid or in a gas.

4. **A physical change** is one where no new chemical is made but the substance acquires new properties, e.g. ice melting.

5. **A chemical change** occurs when a new substance is formed, e.g. magnesium burning in oxygen to form magnesium oxide.

6. An **atom** is the smallest part of an element that can have independent existence.

7. A **molecule** is formed when two or more atoms combine chemically, e.g. H_2O, CO_2.

8. **Sub-atomic particles.**

Particle	Charge	Mass	Position
Proton	+1	1 A.M.U.	in nucleus
Electron	−1	1/1800 A.M.U.	orbits nucleus
Neutron	0	1 A.M.U.	in nucleus

A.M.U. = Atomic Mass Unit.

H 9. The **atomic number** tells how many protons are in the nucleus of an atom. It also tells how many electrons are orbiting the nucleus of an atom. The **mass number** tells us how many protons and neutrons can be found in the nucleus. The **atomic mass minus the atomic number** tells how many neutrons are in the nucleus of an atom, e.g. carbon: atomic number 6, atomic mass 12. Carbon has 6 protons, 6 electrons and 6 neutrons.

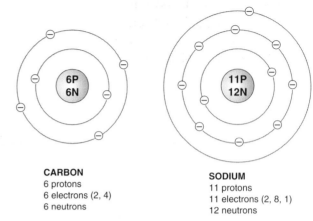

CARBON
6 protons
6 electrons (2, 4)
6 neutrons

SODIUM
11 protons
11 electrons (2, 8, 1)
12 neutrons

Fig. 2.1

H For elements 1-20 only the electrons are organised as follows:

Shell	Number of electrons. Elements 1-20 only
1	2
2	8
3	8
4	2

See example in *Fig. 2.1*.

Questions

1. What is matter? Name the three states of matter.

2. On what does the state of matter depend?

3. What is:
   (a) the melting point of a solid
   (b) the boiling point of a liquid?

4. What is sublimation?
   Name one compound which sublimes.

5. What do you understand by the term 'diffusion'? Give an example.

6. What is:
   (a) a physical change
   (b) a chemical change?

7. Identify the physical and chemical changes in the following list:
   (a) burning magnesium
   (b) mixing salt and sand
   (c) hydrochloric acid added to sodium hydroxide
   (d) iodine subliming.

8. What is:
   (a) an atom
   (b) a molecule?
   Classify the following as atoms or molecules: H, H_2, H_2O, I_2, C, Cl.

9. Name the three subatomic particles found in the atom. Give their mass and charge and say where they are found in the atom.

H 10. What information do we get from:
   (a) the atomic number,
   (b) the atomic mass?

H 11. Draw the Bohr structure of the following atoms:
   (i) He,
   (ii) Mg,
   (iii) P,
   (iv) K.

H 12. What is the electronic configuration of an atom of atomic number:
   (i) 9,
   (ii) 18,
   (iii) 13?
   Identify the three atoms and say how many protons and neutrons each atom has. Classify the three atoms as:
   (a) a metal or a non metal,
   (b) a solid, liquid or gas.

13. Give two pairs of elements, one pair which has the same number of electron shells and a second pair which has the same number of electrons in the outer shell.

Elements, Compounds, Mixtures, Separating Techniques

Key Points

1. An **element** is a substance that cannot be split into simpler substances by chemical means. There are 92 naturally occurring elements which are listed in the periodic table, e.g. copper, hydrogen, nitrogen.

2. A **compound** is a substance which is formed when two or more elements are combined chemically, e.g. H_2O, CO_2.

3. A **mixture** is formed when at least two substances are in contact but are not chemically bonded together, e.g. sea water, air, milk.

4. A **solution** results when one substance **(solute)** dissolves in a second substance **(solvent)**, e.g. sodium chloride (solute) dissolving in water (solvent).

5. When a substance dissolves in a liquid it is said to be **soluble**, e.g. sodium chloride in water.

6. When a substance does not dissolve in a liquid it is said to be **insoluble**, e.g. sand in water.

7. When a small amount of a solute dissolves in a solvent, the solution is said to be **dilute** and when a lot of solute dissolves in a solvent, the solution is **concentrated**.

8. To **separate** a **liquid** from an **insoluble solid**, e.g. sand and water:

    (a) Filter

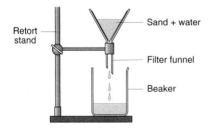

Fig. 2.2

    (b) Decant

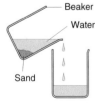

Fig. 2.3

9. To **separate** a **liquid** from a **soluble solid**, e.g. sodium chloride from water:

    (a) Evaporate

    (b) Distil
    Fig. 2.4

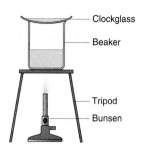

Fig. 2.4

10. To **separate immiscible liquids** (liquids which do not mix), e.g. oil and water. Use a separating funnel.
    Fig. 2.5

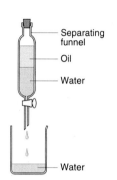

Fig. 2.5

11. To **separate miscible liquids** with **different boiling points**, e.g. ethanol and water. Use distillation.
    Fig. 2.6

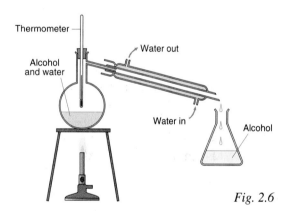

Fig. 2.6

Questions

1. What is an element ? Give three examples.

2. What is the symbol for the following elements? Hydrogen, Sodium, Nitrogen, Sulphur, Aluminium, Helium, Tin, Lead.

3. Some of the symbols of the elements in Q.2 have one letter and some have two letters. Why is this?

4. Some of the symbols do not begin with the initial letter of the element, e.g. the symbol for Sodium is Na. Why is this?

5. Match the element in column 1 with the symbol in column 2:

Hydrogen	C
Calcium	Cl
Chlorine	Ca
Helium	H
Carbon	He

6. Match the use of the element in column 1 with the elements in column 2:

Electric wire	Gold
Test for starch	Oxygen
Kills bacteria in water treatment	Argon
Jewellery	Calcium
Found in air	Copper
Soft drinks can	Iodine
Gas in electric light bulb	Chlorine
Good for bones	Fluorine
Strengthens teeth	Carbon
"Lead" in pencils	Aluminium

7. What is a compound? Give three examples.

8. What is a mixture? Give three examples.

9. State three differences between a mixture and a compound.

10. Classify the following list into:
    (a) element,
    (b) compound,
    (c) mixture:
    sea water, sulphur dioxide, hydrochloric acid, dilute hydrochloric acid, lithium, steel, iron, rust, milk, carbon, poster paint, graphite, bronze, salad dressing.

11. What is a solution? Give three examples.

12. What is a suspension? Give three examples.

13. Explain the following terms:
    (a) dilute solution
    (b) concentrated solution
    (c) soluble
    (d) insoluble
    (e) saturated solution
    (f) unsaturated solution.

14. Name one factor on which the solubility of a substance depends.

15. Describe how you would produce crystals of copper sulphate in the laboratory.

16. Give two examples in each case of mixtures composed of:
    (a) at least two solids
    (b) at least two liquids
    (c) at least two gases
    (d) a gas mixed with a liquid
    (e) a liquid mixed with a solid.

17. This process separates sand and water.
    What is the process called?
    Name another process you could use to separate sand and water.
    What is the name given to the liquid in beaker B?
    Fig. 2.7

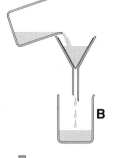

Fig. 2.7

18. Name the piece of apparatus in *Fig. 2.8*.
    Name two liquids that can be separated by this piece of equipment.
    What property must these liquids have?

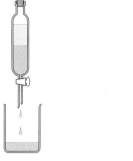

Fig. 2.8

19. What is the name of the process happening in *Fig. 2.9*?
    Name two liquids that can be separated by this process.
    If the two liquids have the same boiling point, can they be separated by this process? Explain.
    Identify the pieces of apparatus X, B and C.
    Why does cold water flow through the piece of apparatus labelled X?
    Is the water tap connected to point Y or Z? Explain.

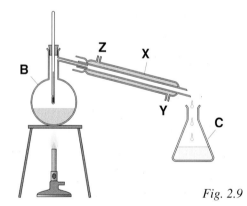

Fig. 2.9

20. How would you separate:
    (a) iron filings and sawdust
    (b) sand and water
    (c) water and alcohol
    (d) oil and water
    (e) salt and water?

The Periodic Table and 'families' of elements

Key Points

1. In the nineteenth century (1869) **Mendeleev** grouped the elements in **increasing atomic weight** and he put elements with similar chemical properties under one another. He had devised a **periodic table**. In the twentieth century **Mosely** placed the elements in **increasing atomic number** rather than atomic weight and he devised the modern periodic table.

2. The periodic table is divided into metals and non-metals.

3. The periodic table contains groups of elements with similar properties.

4. **Group 1 Elements: The Alkali Metals**
   These are the elements of Group 1 of the Periodic Table and include Lithium, Sodium and Potassium.
   They are all soft metals and can be cut with a knife.
   They are all less dense than water and react to give an alkaline solution.
   Lithium burns with a red flame, sodium a yellow flame and potassium with a lilac flame. They all burn to form metallic oxides.

   (H) As one goes from lithium to potassium:
   (1) the reactivity increases, i.e. potassium is more reactive than lithium.
   (2) the atomic number increases.
   (3) the number of electrons in the outer shell is constant – the chemical properties of the elements are similar.
   (4) the number of electron shells increases.

(H) 5. **Group 2 elements** are called the **alkaline earth elements**. They include Beryllium, Calcium, Magnesium and Strontium. They each have two electrons in their outer shell and therefore they have similar chemical properties.

(H) 6. **The Halogens** (Halogen = salt former)
   These are in Group 7 of the Periodic Table and include Fluorine, Chlorine, Bromine and Iodine. They each have seven electrons in their outer shells and they have similar chemical properties. Fluorine and chlorine are gases. Bromine is a liquid and iodine is a solid at room temperature. The halogens are not very soluble in water. Chlorine will dissolve in water as it is used in water treatment and in swimming pools. Reactivity decreases as we go down the group. The halogens react with the alkali metals to form salts, e.g.

   Sodium + chlorine ⟶ Sodium chloride

H 7. **The Noble Gases**

These include Helium, Neon and Argon. These elements are found in Group 8 in the periodic table and they each have a full outer shell. There is no tendency for them to accept, give away or share electrons and there is little tendency for them to form compounds with other elements. The boiling point increases as we go down the group, e.g. helium has a lower boiling point than argon.

Questions

1. Who in the nineteenth century organised the elements into increasing atomic weight? What did he call this table? Why?

2. What name is given to the elements in Group 1 of the Periodic Table?

3. How many electrons do the elements referred to in Q.2 have in their outer shell? Name three of these elements. Give three characteristic properties of these elements. How do these elements react with water?
H Write an equation to show how the second element in this family reacts with water.

4. What colour flame is observed when potassium is burned?
H What part of the air does the potassium react with?
H Write an equation for this reaction.

H 5. How does reactivity vary as one goes down Group 1?

H 6. What name is given to the elements in Group 2 on the Periodic Table? How does calcium react with water? How would you test the solution to see if it is acidic or alkaline?

H 7. What is meant by the term 'halogen'? Name the first three halogen gases in the Periodic Table. How many electrons do these elements have in their outer shell? The first and second numbers of this family are used in water treatment. What is the function of each? Write an equation for the reaction between an alkali metal and a halogen. What type of bond is formed?

H 8. What is special about the outermost shell of the noble gases? Why do they not form many compounds? Name the first three elements in this family and mention one use to which each can be put.

Ions, Bonding, Equations

Key Points

1. An **ion** is an atom which has either a positive or a negative charge, e.g. a sodium ion Na^+. A chloride ion Cl^-.

   $Na \rightarrow Na^+ + e$. Sodium has lost an electron.

   $Cl + e \rightarrow Cl^-$.   Chlorine has gained an electron.

H 2. The **valency** of an element is the number of electrons that an atom will accept, give away or share, so that the element has a full outer shell.

H 3. An **ionic bond** involves transfer of electrons. An ionic bond is formed when one or more electrons are transferred from one atom to another. The resulting ions are held together by the attraction of their opposite charges.

   e.g. $Na^+ + Cl^- \rightarrow NaCl$

H 4. A **covalent bond** involves sharing of electrons. A covalent bond is formed when one or more pairs of electrons are shared between atoms.

Shared pairs	Bond	Example
1	Single	Hydrogen
2	Double	Oxygen
3	Triple	Nitrogen

5. **Ionic compounds:**
   (a) have high melting and boiling points,
   (b) generally dissolve in water,
   (c) conduct electricity when molten or dissolved in water,
   (d) are generally solids at room temperature.

6. **Covalent compounds:**
   (a) have low melting and boiling points,
   (b) are generally insoluble in water,
   (c) do not conduct electricity,
   (d) are generally gases, liquids or soft solids at room temperature.

7. A **radical** is a group of atoms, which have a positive or a negative charge and generally remain bonded together, e.g. SO_4^{-2}, NO_3^-.

8. A balanced equation gives us information about the reactants and the products. It tells us the ratio in which the materials react. The same number of atoms of each type of element should be on each side of the equation.

e.g. $H_2 + O_2 \rightarrow 2 H_2O$.

There are two hydrogen atoms and one oxygen atom on each side of the equation.

Questions

1. What is an ion? Give an example of a positive and a negative ion.

(H) 2. What do you understand by the valency of an element? What is the valency of the following elements? sodium, oxygen, calcium, fluorine, hydrogen, carbon, aluminium.

(H) 3. What is an ionic bond? Give an example of two elements that are held together by an ionic bond. List four properties of ionic compounds.

(H) 4. What is a covalent bond? Give an example of a compound that would exhibit covalent bonding. List four properties that you would expect a covalent compound to have.

(H) 5. What is a radical? Give an example of a positive radical and a negative radical.

(H) 6. What is the formula of the following compounds?

Sodium fluoride	Calcium carbonate
Sodium oxide	Ammonium sulphate
Calcium sulphide	Potassium nitrate
Calcium bromide	Magnesium nitrate
Magnesium chloride	Aluminium sulphate
Sodium hydrogen carbonate	Potassium carbonate

(H) 7. Balance the following equations.

$Mg + O_2 \rightarrow MgO$

$Na + F_2 \rightarrow NaF$

$Li + O_2 \rightarrow Li_2O$

$H_2 + O_2 \rightarrow H_2O$

$H_2O \rightarrow H_2 + O_2$

$H_2SO_4 + Mg \rightarrow MgSO_4 + H_2$

$HNO_3 + Ca \rightarrow Ca(NO_3)_2 + H_2$

$HCl + Ca(OH)_2 \rightarrow CaCl_2 + H_2O$

(H) 8. Complete and balance the following equations:

$HCl + CaCO_3 \rightarrow CaCl_2 + H_2O + CO_2$

$Na + Cl_2 \rightarrow 2NaCl$

$H_2SO_4 + Cu \rightarrow CuSO_4 + H_2$

$HCl + Zn \rightarrow ZnCl_2 + H_2$

$Na + H_2O \rightarrow Na(OH)_2 + H_2$

$C + O_2 \rightarrow CO_2$

$HCl + Na_2CO_3 \rightarrow 2NaCl + H_2O + CO_2$

H 9. Which acid and which base would you react together to obtain the following salts:
   sodium chloride .... lithium nitrate ....
   calcium sulphate .... potassium chloride?
   What is the name of the reaction which occurs between an acid and a base?

Air and Gases

Key Points

1. **Air is a mixture:**
   Composition of air

Component	%
Nitrogen	78
Oxygen	21
Noble Gases	Approx 1
Carbon Dioxide	0.03
Water	Varies
Other	Varies

2. **Oxygen** is prepared by the **reaction of hydrogen peroxide and manganese dioxide**. Manganese dioxide acts as a **catalyst**, that is, a substance which speeds up a chemical reaction without being used up in the reaction. As oxygen is only partially soluble in water, oxygen is collected by the downward displacement of water.

$$2 H_2O_2 \xrightarrow{MnO_2} 2 H_2O + O_2$$

3. **Properties of Oxygen**
   Physical properties: oxygen is a colourless, odourless gas, partially soluble in water and neutral to litmus.
   Chemical properties: oxygen relights a glowing splint. Oxygen reacts with carbon to form carbon dioxide, $C + O_2 \rightarrow CO_2$. Oxygen reacts with sulphur to give sulphur dioxide. $S + O_2 \rightarrow SO_2$.

4. **Uses of Oxygen**
   Oxygen is used in hospitals to assist people to breathe. Divers carry oxygen in tanks. Oxygen is used in steel making and in welding.

5. **Carbon dioxide** is prepared by the **action of hydrochloric acid on calcium carbonate (marble chips)**.

    $HCl + CaCO_3 \rightarrow CaCl_2 + H_2O + CO_2$.

    Being heavier than air, carbon dioxide is collected by upward displacement of air.

6. **Physical properties:** it is a colourless, odourless gas that is heavier than air.

    Chemical properties: carbon dioxide dissolves in water to form carbonic acid which turns blue litmus paper red.

    $H_2O + CO_2 \rightarrow H_2CO_3$.

    Carbon dioxide turns limewater milky.

7. **Uses:** carbon dioxide is the gas in fizzy drinks. It is used in fire extinguishers. Carbon dioxide is one of the raw materials in photosynthesis. Solid carbon dioxide (dry ice) is used as a refrigerant.

8. **Noble Gases:** these include helium, neon and argon. They have a filled outer shell of electrons and therefore they have no tendency to accept share or give away electrons. As a result they are chemically inactive. Helium is lighter than air and is used to fill balloons. Neon is used in street signs and argon is used to full domestic light bulbs to prevent the filament burning out.

9. We use **fuels** as a source of energy. **Fossil fuels** are non-renewable and include coal, turf, oil and gas. They come from dead animals and plants which lived millions of years ago. When fuels burn they use oxygen and they produce heat, carbon dioxide and water vapour. When the supply of oxygen is reduced carbon monoxide is produced. This is a poisonous gas.

10. Because of the smoke and pollution produced by fossil fuels, **smokeless fuels** have been introduced. Coal is processed into smokeless coal by the removal of certain chemicals.

11. **Heat:** a supply of **fuel** and a supply of **air (oxygen)** are necessary for a fire to burn. Firefighters try to control and eliminate one of the three. There are many types of fire extinguisher – water, carbon dioxide, dry powder, foam.

12. Fire hazards should be recognised and precautions taken to avoid the risk of fire. Fire hazards include:
    (i)   leaving a fire without a guard,
    (ii) lighting a fire in a wooded area,
    (iii) overloading electrical sockets.

Questions

1. 'Air is a mixture'. Give two pieces of evidence to show that this statement is true.

2. What are the main components of air? List the percentage of each component of air.

3. Name two components of air of which the percentage varies.

4. Name two materials which you would use to produce oxygen in the laboratory.
   Which of these materials acts as a catalyst?
   What do you understand by the term "catalyst"?

5. Oxygen is collected over water. What does this tell you about the solubility of oxygen in water?

6. What are the physical properties of oxygen?

7. How would you test a gas to show that it was oxygen?

8. What product is formed when oxygen reacts with:
   (a) carbon
   (b) sulphur
   (c) magnesium?

H 9. Write balanced equations for the reactions in Q.8.

10. List three uses of oxygen.

11. How would you prepare carbon dioxide in the laboratory? Draw a labelled diagram of the apparatus you would use.

H 12. Write an equation for the reaction in Q.11.

13. Give three physical properties of carbon dioxide.

14. How would you demonstrate that carbon dioxide is heavier than air?

15. What compound is found when carbon dioxide reacts with water? How would you prove that this compound is an acid?

16. Will things burn in carbon dioxide? On the basis of this, what use can carbon dioxide be put to?

17. What property distinguishes carbon dioxide from other chemicals?

18. Give three uses of carbon dioxide.

19. What unusual property does solid carbon dioxide, 'dry ice' have?

20. Why are the noble gases unreactive?

21. Give one use each of helium, neon and argon.

22. What is a fuel?

23. What do you understand by the term 'fossil fuel'? Name four fossil fuels. Are fossil fuels renewable or non-renewable?

(H) 24. Methane gas is a component of natural gas. Balance the following equation in which methane reacts with oxygen.
$$CH_4 + O_2 \rightarrow H_2O + CO_2$$

25. What gas is produced when carbon burns, where there is a limited supply of oxygen? What is the danger associated with this gas?

26. Give two benefits of using smokeless fuels.

27. What is a fire hazard? Give three examples of fire hazards.

28. Three requirements are necessary for a fire to start and continue burning. What are they?

29. Name four types of fire extinguishers and say what type of fire they are suitable for.

30. What type of fire extinguisher would not be suitable for:
    (a) an electric fire
    (b) a chip pan fire?

Water

Key Points

1. **Formula**: H_2O
   Melting point: $0°C$
   Boiling point: $100°C$
   Maximum density: $4°C$

2. **Surface Tension**: the ability of water to behave as if there was a skin on the surface.
   Examples:
   (i) a drop of water on the end of a glass rod,
   (ii) the ability of a pin or a needle to float on water,
   (iii) water drops are spherical.

3. **Capillarity**: the ability of water to rise through narrow tubes.
   Examples:
   (i) water rising through the xylem of plants,
   (ii) water rising through filter paper.

4. Water is a **good solvent** forming aqueous solutions.

5. **Acid rain:**
   Cause: fumes from the combustion of fuels; rainwater dissolving sulphur dioxide and carbon dioxide which are present in the atmosphere.
   Effect: damages buildings; harmful to plants especially trees; harmful to animals, especially fish; causes respiratory problems in humans.
   Removal: fitting catalytic converters to car exhausts; control the burning of fossil fuels.

6. **Water treatment:**
   (i) **Screening:** removal of large waste materials by passing through a screen.
   (ii) **Settling:** removal of small suspended solids, being more dense than water settle on the bottom of settlement tanks.
   (iii) **Filtration:** water filtered through sand and gravel which removes the remaining suspended solids.
   (iv) **Addition of chemicals:**
   Chlorine: makes water safe to drink by removing pathogenic bacteria.
   Fluorine: sodium fluoride is added which helps to reduce tooth decay.

7. **Soft water** easily forms a lather with soap.
   Hard water does not easily form a lather with soap.
   Types of hardness:
   Temporary hardness which can be removed by boiling.
   Permanent hardness which cannot be removed by boiling

   Cause of hardness of water: salts containing magnesium and calcium ions.
   Temporary hardness; calcium hydrogen carbonate, $Ca(HCO_3)_2$; magnesium hydrogen carbonate, $Mg(HCO_3)_2$.
   Permanent hardness; calcium chloride, $CaCl_2$; calcium sulphate, $CaSO_4$; magnesium chloride, $MgCl_2$; magnesium sulphate, $MgSO_4$.

   Removal of hard water: temporary hardness can be removed by boiling, permanent hardness cannot be removed by boiling.
   Permanent hardness can be removed by passing the water through an ion exchange (resin or zeolite).

Advantages of hard water	Disadvantages of hard water
1. Source of ions for the body e.g. calcium ions for bones. 2. Good for brewing. 3. Nice taste.	1. Wastes soap. 2. Forms a deposit in kettles, saucepans etc. 3. Blocks pipes. 4. Reduces efficiency of radiators. 5. Wastes energy.

Questions

1. What is the formula of water?

2. What do we call the point at which water changes to:
   (i)   a solid
   (ii) a gas?

3. State two uses of:
   (i)   steam
   (ii) ice.

4. How does the volume of water change when it freezes? Identify two problems which occur due to this effect.

5. Match A, B, C ... with 1, 2, 3 ... below:
   A. Boiling Point
   B. Melting Point
   C. Solvent
   D. Surface tension
   E. Capillarity

   1. Will dissolve salt
   2. Water turns to steam
   3. Ice turns to water
   4. Allows a small insect to walk on water
   5. Allows water to move through a plant

6. Identify a gas, a liquid and a solid which dissolve in water.

7. Name two gases which cause acid rain.
   What acids occur in acid rain?
   Are these acids strong or weak?
   Write equations for the formation of these acids.
   Outline the effects of these acids on the environment.
   How can we reduce the production of acid rain?

8. Draw a diagram to illustrate the water cycle.
   In the water cycle, describe two ways that water can get into the atmosphere.
   What does the water form in the atmosphere?
   How does the water get back to the ground?

9. In the purification of water there are four stages: screening, settling, filtration and the addition of chlorine and fluorine. Briefly outline the function of the four stages.
   Describe an experiment to demonstrate stage three.
   What is the purpose of adding chlorine and fluorine to our water supply?
   Why can we not taste the chemicals which are added to the water supply?

10. How would you recognise:
    (i)   soft water
    (ii) hard water?
    What ions cause hardness of water?

Distinguish between:
(i)   temporary hardness and
(ii) permanent hardness.

List three:
(i)   advantages
(ii) disadvantages of hard water?
How would you remove temporary hardness from water?
Can permanent hardness be removed by this method?

H How would you remove permanent hardness from water?

H Write an equation to show what happens when permanent hardness is removed from water.

H 11. A student had four test tubes containing samples of water taken from different locations. He took 2cm³ samples of water and added soap solution until a permanent lather appeared. His experimental results are shown in the table below.

Test Tube	Addition of soap solution to water samples (cm³)	Addition of soap solution after boiling water (cm³)	Addition of soap solution after passing water through an ion exchanger (cm³)
W	2	2	2
X	5	2	2
Y	5	4	2
Z	6	6	2

What type of water was contained in the 4 test tubes?

H 12. A student was given three test tubes containing samples of water, the contents of which are given in the table below.

Test Tube	Contents
X	De-ionised water
Y	De-ionised water plus magnesium hydrogen carbonate
Z	De-ionised water plus magnesium sulphate

Which of the solutions would lather most easily with soap solution?
Identify the types of hardness of water found in the test tubes.
How would you remove the hardness found in the water in the test tubes above?
Name another compound that could be placed in test tube X and one that could be placed in test tube Y to give similar results.

Acids, Bases, pH

Key Points

1. **Acids** turn litmus paper red and they have a sour taste, e.g. lemon juice contains citric acid. Note: testing acids by taste is not a good idea.

2. **Bases** turn litmus paper blue. They feel soapy, e.g. sodium hydroxide, milk of magnesia.

3. A **salt** is formed when the hydrogen of an acid is replaced by a metal.

4. An **indicator** can tell whether a substance is an acid or a base, e.g. litmus is red in acid, blue in base.

5. **pH** is a scale which runs from 0-14. < 7 is acidic, 7 is neutral and > 7 is basic. The stronger the acid, the nearer is the pH to 0 and the stronger the base the nearer is the pH to 14.

6. **Universal indicator** can tell, using a different colour for each pH value, the pH of a substance.

7. Acid + base → salt + water
   Hydrochloric acid + sodium hydroxide → sodium chloride + water.

8. Acid + metal (not all metals) → salt + hydrogen
   Sulphuric acid + zinc → zinc sulphate + hydrogen

9. Acid + metal carbonate → salt + carbon dioxide + water
   Hydrochloric acid + sodium carbonate → sodium chloride + carbon dioxide + water

H 10. **Neutralisation** is the reaction between an acid and a base to give salt and water
   Hydrochloric acid + sodium hydroxide → sodium chloride + water

Questions

1. What do you understand by the terms:
   (i) acid
   (ii) base
   (iii) salt?

2. Name two household items in each case which contain:
   (i) acids *lemon / vinegar*
   (ii) bases. *battery acid oven cleaner*

3. What is an indicator? Name an indicator and say what is its colour in:
   (i) acid *red litmus*
   (ii) base. *blue litmus*

4. A student had three beakers. One contained hydrochloric acid, a second contained sodium hydroxide solution and a third contained distilled water. How could she distinguish between them? *Universal indicator (or litmus)*

5. What is the pH scale?
   A student tested five solutions with universal indicator and her results are tabulated below.

Solution	A *acid*	B *neutral*	C *acid*	D *base*	E *base*
pH	1	7	6	13	10

   What type of solutions were in A-E?

6. Anthocyanin gives red cabbage its colour and also acts as an universal indicator. Outline an experiment to extract this compound from red cabbage. How would you test the resulting solution to test if it is an universal indicator?

7. Write the word equation for the reaction between:
   (a) hydrochloric acid and sodium hydroxide, *hydrochloric acid + sodium hydroxide → sodium chloride + water*
   (b) hydrochloric acid and zinc,
   (c) hydrochloric acid and sodium carbonate.

H 8. Explain what you mean by the term neutralisation.
   A student titrated hydrochloric acid against sodium hydroxide. Explain, using a diagram how this experiment was carried out. Write a balanced equation for the reaction, naming the products. What is the pH of the resulting solution? One of the products of the reaction was a salt. How would you isolate a sample of this salt? Where would you find a sample of this salt in the home?

H 9. Complete and balance the following equations.
   (a) $HCl + Mg \rightarrow$
   (b) $HCl + NaOH \rightarrow$
   (c) $HCl + Na_2CO_3 \rightarrow$
   (d) $H_2SO_4 + NaOH \rightarrow$
   (e) $H_2SO_4 + CaCO_3 \rightarrow$
   (f) $H_2SO_4 + Zn \rightarrow$

Metals

Key Points

1. **Metals** have a **lustre**, i.e. they are shiny, e.g. gold.
   Metals are **malleable** – they can be hammered into sheets, e.g. gold.
   Some metals are **ductile** – they can be drawn out to form wires, e.g. copper.
   Metals are good **conductors** of heat and electricity.

2. An **alloy** is formed when two elements, generally metals, are combined to form a metallic substance. Steel is an alloy formed from a metal and a non-metal, carbon and iron. Brass is an alloy formed from two metals, copper and zinc.

3. Iron and steel combine with oxygen in damp conditions to form rust. Preventative measures include painting, galvanising (coating with zinc), greasing, oiling, electroplating, stainless steel.

(H) 4. **Oxides of metals are basic**, e.g. sodium oxide, and **oxides of nonmetals are acidic**, e.g. carbon dioxide.

(H) 5. The **activity series** is a table of metals, with the most reactive metal (potassium) at the top of the table and least reactive metal (gold) at the bottom, and the other metals placed between potassium and gold according to their reactivity.

(H) 6. Generally metals are found combined with other substances and they have to be extracted from their ore. The method of extraction depends on the metal's position on the activity series. Metals closer to the bottom of the series are easier to extract than those at the top of the series.

(H) 7. **Corrosion of metals** is caused by the action of oxygen, water or other chemicals and metals at the top of the activity series are more susceptible to corrosion than those at the bottom of the series.

8. **A simple cell** consists of a zinc electrode (anode), and a copper electrode (cathode) placed in an electrolyte, e.g. sulphuric acid. The electrodes are connected to the terminals of a bulb or a voltmeter. A voltage of approximately 1.1v max. is produced when the electrodes are copper and zinc.
   Fig. 2.10

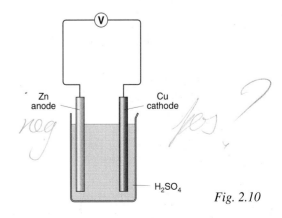

Fig. 2.10

H 9. If different sets of electrodes are used in a simple cell different voltages are obtained. The further away they are from one another on the activity series of metals the larger the voltage obtained.

H 10. The **dry cell** consists of a zinc case which is the cathode, a carbon rod covered with a metal cap which acts as the anode and electrolyte is a paste of ammonium chloride.

H 11. **Electrolysis of water** is the splitting of water into its elements by means of an electric current, using a Hoffman Voltameter. The electrodes are platinum and the water is acidulated to facilitate the flow of current.
Fig. 2.11
Anode reaction: $2OH^- \rightarrow H_2O + 2e + O_2$
Cathode reaction: $H^+ + e \rightarrow H_2$
Net reaction: $H_2O \rightarrow H_2 + O_2$

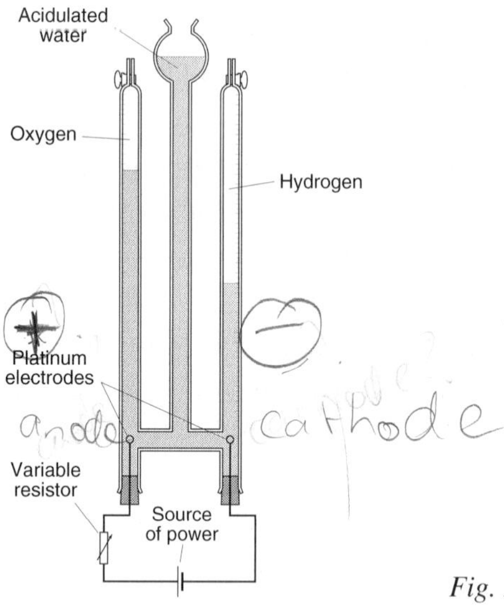

Acidulated water

Oxygen

Hydrogen

Platinum electrodes

Variable resistor

Source of power

Fig. 2.11

12. **Electroplating** is the deposition of one metal on another. It is used to protect or to decorate other metals, e.g. silver plating (EPNS electro plated nickel silver), chrome plating. The object to be plated is placed at the cathode of the electroplating cell and the anode is made of the metal to be plated. The electrolyte is a solution of a salt made from the metal to be plated.
Fig. 2.12

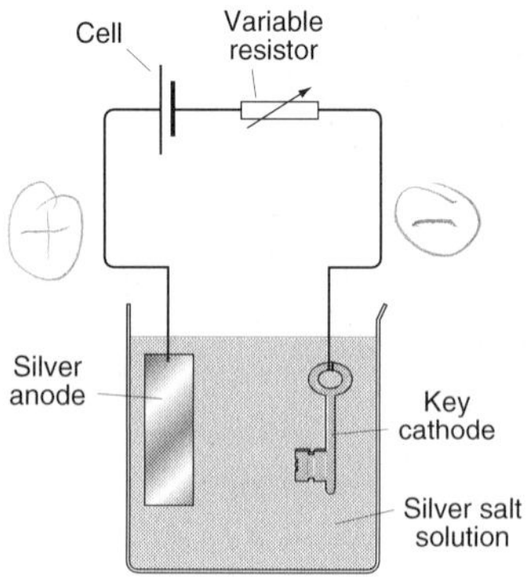

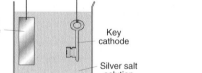

Cell   Variable resistor

Silver anode

Key cathode

Silver salt solution

Fig. 2.12

Questions

1. What is a metal?

2. Metals are said to be **malleable**, **ductile** and have a **lustre**.
   Explain the above words.

3. What is:
   (i) a conductor
   (ii) an insulator?

4. You are given bars of copper, zinc, glass, plastic. How would you show that some of these bars conduct electricity and some do not?

5. What is an alloy? Why are alloys important? Name one alloy composed of a metal and a non-metal and one alloy composed of two metals. Name the elements in each alloy. Give one use for each alloy you have mentioned.

6. Rust is one of the main drawbacks of using iron or steel. What is rust? Suggest five methods of preventing rust and give an example of where each method is used. Is rusting an oxidation or reduction reaction? Explain.

H 7. How would you test to see if oxides of metals and oxides of non-metals are acidic or basic? What result should you get?

H 8. What is the activity series of metals? Place the following groups of metals in increasing order of reactivity:
   (i) Au, Na, Cu, Zn.
   (ii) K, Ag, Fe, Cu.

H 9. Place the following list of elements in decreasing order of reactivity:
   Au, Na, Zn, Cu, Ag, K, Fe.

H 10. What is an ore?

H 11. What is meant by metals corroding?
   How may this process be slowed down?

H 12. Describe how you would determine whether copper or iron corrodes more quickly.

13. What is the function of a simple cell? Using a diagram, describe how you would construct a simple cell.
    What metals would you use for the electrodes?
    What electrolyte would you use?
    How would you measure the voltage output from such a cell?
    What would you notice occurring at the anode?

H 14. Why is the dry cell more convenient to use that the simple cell?
    Describe the dry cell.
    Give two advantages and two disadvantages of using dry cells.

H 15. What is the name of the piece of apparatus used in the electrolysis of water?
    Why is the water acidulated?
    From what are the electrodes made?
    Write an equation to show what happens at the anode and cathode.
    Which gas is collected at:
    (a) the anode,
    (b) the cathode?
    In the electrolysis of water, 3.5cm³ of gas was collected at the cathode. How much gas was collected at the anode? Explain.
    Write an equation to show the net result of the electrolysis of water.

16. What do you understand by the term electroplating?
    Mention two purposes of electroplating.
    An electroplating cell is set up to plate copper onto iron nails:
    what is the anode made from?
    Name a suitable electrolyte.
    What happens at the cathode?
    Draw a suitable circuit for the electroplating process.
    Is this an oxidation or a reduction reaction? Explain.
    Is AC or DC current used?

H 17. In two simple cells the following pairs of electrodes are used:
    (i) copper and iron
    (ii) zinc and copper.
    Which cell will produce the greatest voltage? Explain.

H 18. Write balanced equations for the following:
    (i) The reaction of sodium with water.
    (ii) The reaction of magnesium with dilute hydrochloric acid.
    (iii) The reaction of copper and oxygen.
    In each case say what would be observed when the above reactions take place.

H 19. How do sodium, zinc and iron react with:
(i) oxygen
(ii) water
(iii) dilute acid?
Write balanced equations in each case and as a result place the elements in increasing order of reactivity.

H 20. Sodium chloride (table salt) and sucrose (table sugar) both dissolve in water but only sodium chloride solution conducts electricity. Explain.

Oxidation/Reduction

Key Points

1. **Oxidation** occurs when a substance combines with oxygen in a chemical reaction.
   Reduction occurs when a substance loses oxygen in a chemical reaction.

H 2. Oxidation is the loss of electrons and reduction is the gain of electrons.
(OIL RIG: oxidation is loss, reduction is gain).

H 3. Oxidation is the loss of hydrogen in a chemical reaction and reduction is the gain of hydrogen in a chemical reaction.

H 4. An **exothermic reaction** is one where heat is given out during a chemical reaction, e.g. magnesium burning to form magnesium oxide.

H 5. An **endothermic reaction** is one where heat is taken in during a chemical reaction, e.g. the addition of ammonium chloride to water.

Questions

1. What is understood by the terms:
   (i) oxidation
   (ii) reduction?

H 2. What is oxidation in terms of loss or gain of:
   (i) oxygen
   (ii) hydrogen
   (iii) electrons?

3. Which of the following reactions could be considered to be oxidation reactions? In the case(s) where oxidation or reduction occurs, say which species is:
   (i) oxidised
   (ii) reduced.

   $K + Cl_2 \rightarrow KCl$

   $2Li + O_2 \rightarrow Li_2O$

   $AgNO_3 + KCl \rightarrow AgCl + KNO_3$

   $Zn + CuSO_4 \rightarrow ZnSO_4 + Cu$

   $SO_3 + O_2 \rightarrow SO_3$

4. Is it possible to have oxidation with reduction? Explain your answer.

5. What is:
   (a) an exothermic reaction
   (b) an endothermic reaction?
   Give an example of each.

Chapter 3   BIOLOGY

Animal Biology: Introduction

There are many different animals on the earth. They are grouped into families. Animals exhibit the seven characteristics of life: movement, feeding, respiration, sensitivity, excretion, growth, reproduction.

Animals are important to humans as they are a source of food, e.g. agriculture and mariculture. They are as a source of medicine, e.g. insulin, and they are also used in drug development. Many leisure activities are concerned with animals: horse riding and racing, keeping pets, zoos.

Cells

Key Points

1. Plants and animals are made of **cells** which are the basic unit of life.

2. **Animal cells** are composed of:
    Cell membrane keeps the parts of the cell together and allows **oxygen** and **food** into the cell, and **carbon dioxide** and **water** out of the cell.
    The **nucleus** controls the cell and it contains genetic material.
    Vacuoles contain food and waste products of cell metabolism.
    Cytoplasm is everything within the cell membrane except the nucleus.
    Fig. 3.1

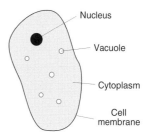

Fig. 3.1

3. **Plant cells** are composed of:
    (In addition to the components found in the animal cell), the **cell wall** protects the cell and gives it support. It contains cellulose.
    Vacuole contains water and helps to give the cell its rigidity.
    The chloroplast contains chlorophyll necessary for photosynthesis.
    Fig. 3.2

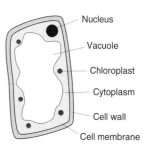

Fig. 3.2

Human Digestive System

Key Points

1. **Food** is a fuel which the body burns to give **energy**. It is also used for **growth** and **repair**.

2. Constituents of the **diet:**
   (a) **Carbohydrates** are found in potatoes, bread, rice, pasta. They contain the elements carbon, hydrogen and oxygen. They are used for energy and they are broken down to sugars in the body.
   (b) **Proteins** are found in meat, fish, dairy products. They contain the elements carbon, hydrogen, oxygen and nitrogen. They are used for growth and repair and they are broken down to amino acids.
   (c) **Fats** are found in fatty meat, oils, butter. They contain the elements carbon, hydrogen and oxygen. They are used for energy and they are broken down to glycerol and fatty acids.
   (d) **Vitamins and minerals** are needed by the body in small amounts to keep healthy. **Vitamin A** is found in carrots. **Vitamin C** is found in citrus fruits. The **mineral** calcium is found in milk and is needed for healthy bones. Iron is found in liver and is used in red blood corpuscles.
   (e) **Fibre** is not digested but assists the digestion process. Sources include cereals, brown bread, raw vegetables.
   (f) **Water**.

3. The energy that we require every day depends on our sex, age and occupation, and the type of activities that we participate in. Different food types have different energy contents.

4. A balanced diet is one where there is adequate amounts of each type of food. **Lack** of a particular constituent in the diet results in health problems such as **malnutrition**.

5. There are five stages in the process:
   (a) **ingestion**   (b) **digestion**   (c) **absorption**   (d) **assimilation**   (e) **egestion**

   (a) **Ingestion** is taking food into the body by the mouth. The food is chopped up by the teeth and mixed with saliva. Saliva contains an enzyme, salivary amylase, which starts the digestion of starch to sugar.
   (b) **Digestion** is the breaking down of the food into molecules which the body can use. The body uses enzymes for this process. Digestion occurs in the mouth, the stomach and the small intestine.
   (c) **Absorption** occurs in the small intestine where the digested food passes into the bloodstream so that it can be taken to all parts of the body.

(d) **Assimilation** occurs when the food molecules become part of the body.

(e) **Egestion** occurs when undigested food is passed out of the body via the anus (*note, this is not excretion*).

The Teeth

Key Points

1. There are four types of teeth in a human being – **incisors**, **canines**, **premolars**, **molars**.
   The **incisors** bite food.
   The **canines** tear food (these teeth are well developed in carnivores, e.g. dogs and lions).
   The **premolars** and **molars** grind up the food.
   The type of teeth we have is dependent on our diet, e.g. a herbivore (a sheep) does not have well developed canines. *Fig. 3.3*

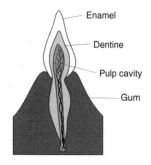

Fig. 3.3

(H) 2. The **end products of digestion**
   Carbohydrates are broken down to sugars.
   Proteins are broken down to amino acids.
   Fats are broken down to fatty acids and glycerol.

(H) 3. **Enzymes** are complex chemicals which break down foods to simple molecules. They are produced in the mouth, stomach, pancreas and the small intestine. Amylase breaks down starch to sugar.

4. The **mouth** breaks up food physically. The digestion of starch by the enzyme amylase begins.
   The **oesophagus** is the tube which brings the food from the mouth to the stomach.
   The **stomach** is where protein digestion begins. The contents of the stomach are acidic. Food is churned up by the stomach muscles.
   The **small intestine** is where the digestion of carbohydrates, proteins and fats is completed. The digested food is absorbed into the bloodstream.
   The **large intestine** is where water is reabsorbed into the body.
   Faeces are stored in the **rectum**.
   Undigested food is egested from the body at the **anus**.
   Anatomy of the digestive system. Fig 3.4

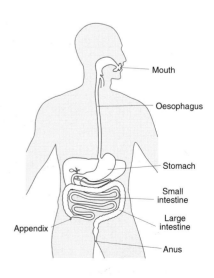

Fig. 3.4

The Respiratory System

Key Points

1. **Energy** is required by all living organisms.

2. **Respiration** is the **release of energy** from food using oxygen.

3. When a person breathes, **oxygen** is taken into the body by the lungs. **Carbon dioxide** and **water vapour** are expired from the body.

4. The **respiratory system** consists of:

    (a) the **nose**: where air is filtered and warmed.
    (b) the **mouth**: air is also taken in here.
    (c) the **epiglottis**: stops food and drink entering the lungs.
    (d) the **trachea**: connects the mouth and nose to the bronchi.
    (e) the **bronchi**: connects the trachea to each lung.
    (f) **rings of cartilage**: keeps the trachea and bronchi open.
    (g) **alveoli**: where gas exchange takes place.
    (h) **ribs**: protect the lungs and assist in the breathing process.
    (i) **diaphragm**: is a sheet of muscle which assists in the breathing process.
    (j) the respiratory system is lined with **mucus** and **tiny hairs** which **filter and clean** the incoming air.

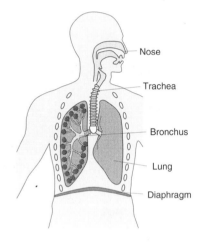

Fig. 3.5

5. **Smoking**:
    (a) may cause lung cancer.
    (b) may cause heart disease and lung disease.
    (c) produces toxic gases which affect the smoker and other people (**passive smoking**).
    (d) gives people smoker's cough.

Transport/Circulatory System

Key Points

1. Composition and function of the **blood**:
    (a) **Red blood corpuscles** contain red coloured haemoglobin. Iron is necessary in the diet for the production of haemoglobin. **Haemoglobin** carries oxygen around the body. There are approximately 5 million red blood corpuscles/cm³ blood and they are made in the bone marrow.
    (b) There are 4,000-10,000 **white blood cells**/cm³ blood. They fight disease and they are also made in the bone marrow.
    (c) **Platelets** cause the blood to clot when the body gets a cut, otherwise the body would bleed to death. The clotting factor is missing in haemophiliacs.
    (d) **Plasma** is the liquid in which all the components of the blood are found. It carries food and carbon dioxide around the body.

2. **Blood vessels:**
    Arteries carry blood away from the heart. They normally carry oxygenated blood, the exception being the pulmonary artery which carries deoxygenated blood to the lungs. Arteries have thick walls and a pulse.

    Ⓗ Oxygenated blood is bright red and deoxygenated blood is dark red.

    Veins carry blood back to the heart from the body. They normally carry deoxygenated blood with the exception of the pulmonary vein which carries oxygenated blood from the lungs to the heart.

    Ⓗ Veins have thin walls. They have valves to assist the blood to flow in one direction against gravity from the legs to the heart.

    Capillaries join the arteries to the veins. They allow exchange of various chemicals (e.g. food, oxygen, carbon dioxide) with the body cells.

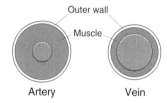

Fig. 3.6

3. The **heart** is a muscular pump which pumps blood around the body. The muscle of the right side of the heart is thinner than the muscle of the left side of the heart, because the left side of the heart pumps blood to the whole body, whereas the right side of the heart pumps blood only to the lungs.

4. **Care of the heart.**
    (a) Do not become overweight.
    (b) Do not smoke.
    (c) Keep to a low fat diet.
    (d) Reduce your level of stress.

5. Structure of the heart and circulatory system.
   Fig. 3.7

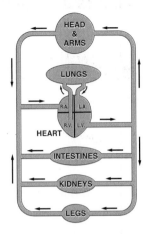

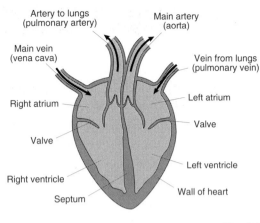

Fig. 3.7

Excretory System

Key Points

1. **Excretion** is the removal of waste materials from the cells of the body.

2. There are three excretory organs:
   (a) The **lungs** get rid of carbon dioxide and water vapour.
   (b) The **skin** gets rid of water, salts and some urea.
   (c) The **kidneys** get rid of urine (water and urea). **Urea** is a waste product produced by the breakdown of protein. *Fig. 3.8*

(H) 3. The blood enters the kidneys via the **renal arteries**. The blood is filtered, and the filtered blood is taken back to the heart by the **renal vein**. The urine is taken to the bladder by the ureter. Here the urine is stored. When the bladder is full the urine is expelled from the body by the urethra.

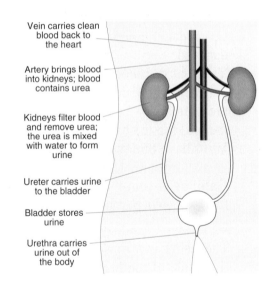

Fig. 3.8

	Function
Ureter	carries blood from the kidney to the bladder
Bladder	stores urine
Urethra	takes urine from the bladder to outside the body

Skeletal System

Key Points

1. The skeleton has three main functions:
   (a) **Support**
   (b) **Movement** – muscles and bones enable us to move.
   (c) **Protection** – examples, the skull protects the brain and the ribs protect the heart and lungs.

2. **Joints:** A joint is where two bones meet.
   Types of joint:
   (a) **Ball and socket joint**, e.g. hip, shoulder.
   (b) **Hinge joint**, e.g. knee.
   (c) **Gliding joint**, e.g. wrist.
   (d) **Pivot joint**, e.g. between the skull and the vertebral column.
   (e) **Fused joint**, e.g. found in the skull.

3. Joints have a lubricating fluid called **synovial fluid**, and the ends of the bones are covered with **cartilage**.

4. Bones are attached to one another by **ligaments**, and muscles are attached to bones by **tendons**.

5. Muscles act by contracting. They work in pairs called **antagonistic pairs**, e.g. the biceps raises the forearm and the triceps lowers the forearm. When one of the pair of muscles contracts, the other muscle relaxes and vice versa.

Sensitivity and Co-ordination

Key Points

1. Humans have five senses.

Organ	Function
skin	touch
eye	sight
ear	hearing
nose	smell
tongue	taste

The sense organs communicate with the brain by **nerves**.

H 2. A **sensory nerve** carries messages from the sense organ to the brain and a **motor nerve** carries messages from the brain to a muscle.

H 3. The **endocrine system** consists of a series of glands in the body which release chemicals called hormones into the blood stream. The endocrine system is not as fast as the **nervous system** but the action of the endocrine system is more sustained (longer lasting), e.g. the hormone **insulin** controls the level of sugar in the blood. Insulin is produced in the pancreas and a lack of this hormone in the body causes diabetes.

4. Parts of the eye. *Fig 3.9*

   (a) The **retina** is a light sensitive layer where the image is formed.

   (b) The **lens** focuses the image onto the retina.

   (c) The **optic nerve** carries the information from the eye to the brain.

   (d) A **blind spot** is where the optic nerve leaves the eye, it contains no light receptors.

   (e) The **fovea** or **yellow spot** is the point of sharpest vision.

   (f) **Vitreous humour** is a jelly like substance which gives the eye its shape. It allows light to pass through.

   (g) **Aqueous humour** gives the front of the eye its shape.

   (h) The **pupil** is a hole in the front of the eye which allows light into the eye.

   (i) The **iris** is the coloured part of the eye which regulates the size of the pupil.

   (j) The **sclerotia** is the 'white' of the eye – this is a tough material which protects the eye.

   (k) The **choroid** is a pigmented layer which stops internal reflection of light in the eye.

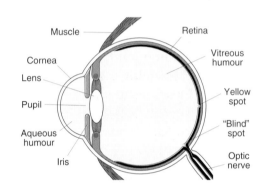

Fig. 3.9

Respiration

Key Points

1. This is the process where **energy is released from food** for use in the body. Oxygen is used in the respiration process and water and carbon dioxide are products of respiration.

   Food + oxygen → carbon dioxide + water + energy.

H 2. $C_6H_{12}O_6 + 6O_2$ → $6CO_2 + 6H_2O$ + energy.

Reproduction and Inheritance

Key Points

1. **Reproduction** is the process where new individuals are produced.

2. The **female reproductive system** produces eggs and carries the developing foetus until birth.
    Fig. 3.10

    (a) **Eggs** are produced in the ovary.
    (b) **Fallopian tubes** carry the egg to the uterus (womb). Fertilisation occurs in the fallopian tubes.
    (c) The **foetus** develops in the uterus.
    (d) **Sperm** enters the woman's body through the **vagina**, and the baby is also born through the vagina.

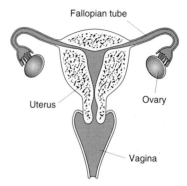

Fig. 3.10

3. The **male reproductive system** produces **sperm**.
    Fig. 3.11

    (a) **Sperm** are produced in the **testes**. The testes are held in a sack called the **scrotum**. The scrotum is outside the body so that the testes are at a lower temperature than the body.
    (b) **Sperm ducts** carry the sperm from the testes to the penis, which is capable of transferring sperm into the body of the female.

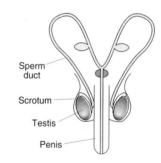

Fig. 3.11

4. **Intercourse** occurs when the male's penis is inserted into the vagina, and sperm are released.

5. **Fertilisation** occurs when the sperm and the egg unite to become a **zygote**.

6. **Pregnancy** is when the baby develops in the uterus of the female. Pregnancy lasts nine months in humans.

7. **Birth** occurs after approximately nine months, when the muscles of the uterus contract and push the baby out through the vagina.

8. The **menstrual cycle** begins by the lining of the uterus breaking down and is expelled through the vagina. This is known as **menstruation** and it lasts approximately five days. The lining of the uterus regenerates and is ready for possible implantation of a zygote. The woman's most fertile period is just after ovulation which occurs from approx. day 13-15 of the cycle. If fertilisation does not occur, the lining of the uterus breaks down and the lining is expelled and the cycle begins again. If fertilisation occurs, the zygote is implanted into the wall of the uterus where it develops. Menstruation then ceases until after the birth of the baby.

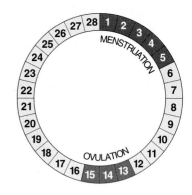

Fig. 3.12

9. **Contraception** is the prevention of fertilisation.

   Methods:
   (a) No intercourse occurs.
   (b) No intercourse occurs during the fertile period.
   (c) Barrier method, e.g. use of a condom.
   (d) Use of a birth control pill.

H **Inheritance**

H 1. This is the **transfer of characteristics** from parent to child, and it is the reason why children resemble their parents.

H 2. Some characteristics are inherited, e.g. eye colour and some characteristics are acquired, e.g. a way of speaking.

H 3. The male and female **gametes** are called the sperm and the egg respectively. These gametes contain **chromosomes** and in the human each gamete contains 23 chromosomes.

H 4. The **chromosomes** are made up of **genes** which are made up of deoxyribonucleic acid **(DNA)**.

H 5. **Eye colour** is an inherited characteristic.
   The gene for brown eyes is dominant and the gene for blue eyes is recessive.
   Each gamete contains a pair of genes.
   B = brown eyes (dominant)
   b = blue eyes (recessive)

Possible combinations of gene pairs.

Combinations of gene pairs	Colour
BB	Brown
Bb	Brown
bb	Blue

Possible combinations of gametes:

BB x BB	Bb x Bb
BB x Bb	Bb x bb
BB x bb	bb x bb

Example: *Fig. 3.13*

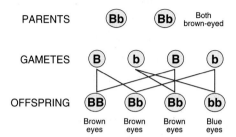

Fig. 3.13

Questions

Nutrition

1. Why do we eat?

2. Name the seven constituents of the diet.
   What is the function of each constituent in the diet?
   Name a source of each type of food.

3. What is a balanced diet?

4. Give one:
   (a) disadvantage
   (b) advantage of dieting.

5. People require different amounts of energy to live a healthy life. List three factors on which the energy needs of the body depend.

6. What is meant by malnutrition? Is it possible for somebody living in Ireland to be malnourished? Explain your answer.

7. Name four different types of tooth found in the human mouth.
   What is the function of each type of tooth?
   How can we prevent tooth decay?

8. Distinguish between chemical and mechanical digestion.

9. There are five stages in the digestive process. List these stages in order, and briefly describe what happens at each stage.

H 10. What are (a) carbohydrates (b) fats and (c) proteins broken down to in the body?

H 11. A student set out to investigate the action of the enzyme which is found in saliva on starch. Name three types of food that are rich in starch.
What is an enzyme? Name the enzyme found in saliva which breaks down starch.
The student kept the test tubes at 37°C throughout the experiment. Why?
When the enzyme acted on the starch, what product was formed? How would you test for this product? Would you expect any starch to be present at the end of the experiment? Explain.

12. In the diagram label the parts A-F and give the function of each part.
Fig. 3.14

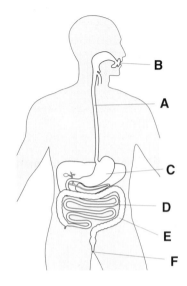

Fig. 3.14

Respiratory System

1. Define respiration. What gas is consumed and what gases are released during respiration?

2. What is the function of the respiratory system in animals?

3. Write a word equation to show what happens during respiration.

H 4. Complete the following equation:
$C_6H_{12}O_6 + 6O_2$

5. Distinguish between inspired and expired air.

6. "Inspired air contains no carbon dioxide and expired air contains no oxygen." Is this statement true or false? Explain your answer.

7. What is shown by the experiment illustrated in *Fig. 3.15*?
What does lime water test for? What does this signify?
Describe the appearance of the lime water in both conical flasks at the end of the experiment.

8. How would you demonstrate that carbon dioxide and water vapour are expired by the lung?

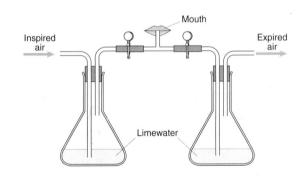

Fig. 3.15

9. Animals have different structures for absorbing oxygen into their bodies. Match the following list of animals with the organ of gas exchange:

Gills	Grasshopper
Skin	Badger
Lungs	Frog
Spiracles	Trout

Do any of the animals above have more than one method for obtaining oxygen? Explain.

10. What is the role of the nose in breathing?

11. Why is it better to breathe through the nose rather than through the mouth?

12. Label the parts A-E ... shown in *Fig. 3.16*.

13. What is the function of the rings of cartilage in the trachea?

14. Explain the function of the epiglottis.

15. Explain the role of the:
    (a) diaphragm,
    (b) rib cage,
    (c) intercostal muscles in breathing.

16. What is the function of the larynx?

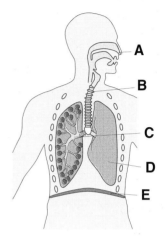

Fig. 3.16

17. How would you construct a model of the respiratory system in the laboratory?

18. In what part of the lungs does gas exchange take place?

19. By what method does gas exchange take place in the lungs?

20. What system transports the oxygen to all parts of the body?

21. What type of blood vessel is in direct contact with the alveoli?

22. What methods are used by the respiratory system to clean the incoming air?

23. "Smoking is said to be one of the greatest health hazards to our lungs". Describe the effect of smoking on the lungs. List four reasons why this statement is true.

24. Describe an experiment to demonstrate an effect of smoking on our lungs.

25. Explain the term aerobic exercise. Give four examples of this type of exercise.

Circulatory System
1. There are four components of the blood. Name them and give one function of each component.

2. What is the function of:
   (a) arteries
   (b) veins
   (c) capillaries?

3. What is the function of the heart?

4. List four ways in which we can reduce our risk of heart disease.

(H) 5. Why do arteries have thicker walls than veins?

6. Which blood vessels carry blood:
   (a) away from the heart
   (b) back to the heart?

7. What is a valve? Which blood vessels have valves?

8. Which blood vessels carry:
   (a) oxygenated blood
   (b) deoxygenated blood?
   There is one exception in each case to this. What is it and why does it arise?

9. What is the function of capillaries in the body?

(H) 10. Name the four chambers in the heart?

11. What is a pulse? Describe how you would take somebody's pulse.

(H) 12. Label the parts of the heart in the diagram.
    Fig 3.17

(H) 13. One side of the heart has thicker walls than the other. Which side is this and why does it have thicker walls?

(H) 14. How would you determine the effect of exercise on heart rate?

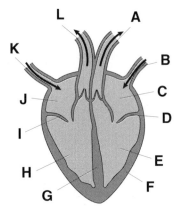

Fig. 3.17

Excretion
1. What is meant by excretion?

2. There are three excretory organs in the body. Name them and say what each excretes.

3. Where is urea produced in the body?

H 4. The following are parts of the excretory system. Give the function of each part:
   (a) renal artery
   (b) renal vein
   (c) ureter
   (d) urethra
   (e) bladder.

Skeletal system

1. Name an animal with an:
   (i) endoskeleton
   (ii) exoskeleton.
   What type of skeleton does a human have?

2. The skeleton has three main functions. What are they?

3. What is a joint? There are five types of joint in the human body. What are they and where is each found?

4. What is:
   (a) cartilage
   (b) synovial fluid, and state what is the function of each?

5. What is a:
   (a) tendon
   (b) ligament?

6. Explain what is meant by an antagonistic pair and say where in the body such a pair may be found?

Sensitivity and co-ordination

1. Humans have five senses. What are they? Name an organ associated with each sense.

H 2. What is the difference between a sensory and a motor nerve?

H 3. What is the endocrine system? List two differences between the endocrine system and the nervous system.

H 4. Name one hormone and say what is its function in the human body?

H 5. In the diagram of the human eye, label the parts A-H.
   Fig. 3.18

H 6. What is the function of each of the following parts of the eye?
   (a) lens   (b) retina
   (c) optic nerve   (d) iris
   (e) pupil

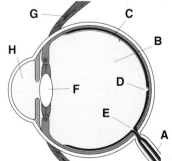

Fig. 3.18

(H) 7. Why is the choroid pigmented?

(H) 8. How would you find your blind spot?

Reproduction

1. Why do we reproduce?

2. In the female:
   (a) Where are eggs produced?
   (b) Where does fertilisation take place?
   (c) What is the function of the uterus?
   The vagina has two functions. What are they?

3. In the male:
   (a) Where are the sperm produced?
   (b) Why are the testes in the scrotum outside the body?
   (c) What is a sperm duct?
   (d) What function does the penis play in reproduction?

4. What is a zygote?

5. How long does pregnancy last in humans?

6. Briefly describe what happens at birth.

7. What happens during the first five days (approx.) of the menstrual cycle?
   What is ovulation and when approx. does it happen in the menstrual cycle?
   What happens if fertilisation:
   (a) takes place
   (b) does not take place?

8. What is contraception?

9. Why do children resemble their parents?
   Give two examples of characteristics which are
   (a) acquired
   (b) inherited.

10. If the gene for brown eyes is dominant over the gene for blue eyes, what colour eyes would the children of parents who both had the gene pairs Bb?
    How many brown eyed and blue eyed children would they have?

11. Is it possible for two parents with blue eyes to have brown eyed children? Explain.

Plants: Introduction

1. There are many different types of plants. They are living organisms and they exhibit the characteristics of life: movement, respiration, feeding, growth, reproduction, excretion, sensitivity to their environment.

2. Uses of plants.
    (a) They recycle oxygen.
    (b) They are a food source.
    (c) They are used in medicine.
    (d) Many useful products are produced from plants, e.g. timber, linen, paper, coffee, tea.
    (e) Plants provide us with many leisure activities, e.g. gardening, walking in the countryside.

3. Plants may be recognised by their distinctive flowers and leaves.

4. Generally a plant has a root, stem, leaves, flowers and stems.
    Fig. 3.19

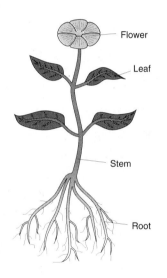

Structure	Function
Root	(a) anchors the plant. (b) absorbs water and minerals from the ground. (c) stores food.
Leaves	(a) make food (photosynthesis) (b) gases diffuse into and out of the leaves. (CO_2, O_2 and H_2O)
Flowers	reproduction
Stems	(a) transport water and minerals from the root to the leaves. (b) transport food to the root for storage.

Fig. 3.19

Plant Nutrition

Key Points

1. **Photosynthesis** is the process by which green plants make their food. Carbon dioxide and water are the new materials. Sunlight provides the energy and the green pigment, **chlorophyll**, traps the sun's energy. Oxygen and starch (food) are produced. This replaces the oxygen which is used up in respiration.

2.

$$\text{Carbon dioxide + water} \xrightarrow{\text{energy/chlorophyll}} \text{Food + oxygen}$$

(H) 3. $6CO_2 + 6H_2O \xrightarrow[\text{chlorophyll}]{\text{energy}} C_6H_{12}O_6 + 6O_2$

(H) 4. Plants need **minerals** for healthy growth. These include **nitrogen**, **phosphorous**, **potassium** and others. If plants do not get sufficient minerals they will not grow well and they will not photosynthesise properly.

(H) 5. To test to see if photosynthesis has occurred, test the leaf for starch. **If starch is present photosynthesis has occurred.**
To test the leaf for starch:
   (a) Boil the leaf to soften it.
   (b) Boil the leaf in alcohol to remove the chlorophyll.
   (c) Drop iodine solutions onto the leaf. If the leaf turns blue/black starch is present and photosynthesis has taken place.

Transport in plants

Key Points

(H) 1. A transport system is necessary in plants to bring water and minerals from the roots to the leaves (through the **xylem**) and food from the leaves to the root for storage (through the **phloem**).

(H) 2. **Transpiration** is the process by which water evaporates from the leaves of plants. There are tiny holes in the leaves of plants called **stoma** which allow water out into the atmosphere.

(H) 3. Factors which affect transpiration:
   (a) **Temperature**: a hot day increases the rate of transpiration.
   (b) **Wind**: a breeze will remove water vapour from around the leaf. More water vapour will replace it so that the rate of transpiration is higher than on a calm day with very little wind.
   (c) **Humidity**: high humidity with a lot of water vapour in the atmosphere lowers the rate of transpiration. Low humidity raises the rate of transpiration.

Responsiveness

Key Points

1. A **tropism** is the response of a plant to a stimulus.

2. **Phototropism** is the response of the plant to light. Stems and leaves are positively phototropic, they grow towards the light. Roots are negatively phototropic, they grow away from the light.
   Fig. 3.20

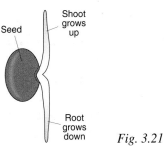
Fig. 3.20

H 3. **Geotropism** is the response of a plant to gravity. The roots are positively phototropic and the stems are negatively phototropic.
   Fig. 3.21

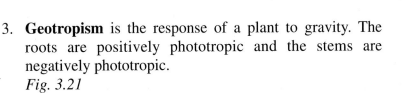
Fig. 3.21

4. Plants are **living organisms** and they **respire**.
   Respiration is the controlled release of energy from food using oxygen. Carbon dioxide, water and energy are produced. (*See section on Respiration, page 60.*)

Reproduction in plants

Key Points

1. **Reproduction** is the way plants produce new organisms similar to themselves.

2. Plant reproduction may be **asexual** or **sexual**.
   Asexual reproduction involves one parent only without the union of gametes. Examples include cuttings and strawberry runners.
   Sexual reproduction involves the union of two gametes, one from each parent. In the case of plants the pollen is the male cell and the egg is the female cell.

3. The **flower is the organ of reproduction** of the plant.
   Parts of the flower.
   The **sepal** protects the flower when it is a bud.
   The **petal** attracts insects to the flower for pollination.
   The **carpel** is the female part of the flower and it produces the egg.

4. The **stamen** is the male part of the flower and it produces the pollen. The **carpel** is the female part of the flower and it consists of the **stigma**, the **style** and the **ovary**. Pollen lands on the stigma, a pollen tube grows down through the style to the ovary (where the egg is produced).
Fig. 3.22
The stamen is the male part of the plant and consists of the **anther** and **filament**. The anther produces pollen.
Fig. 3.23

Fig. 3.22

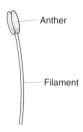

Fig. 3.23

5. There are four stages in the sexual reproduction of plants.
   (a) **Pollination** is the transfer of pollen from the anther of one flower to the stigma of a second flower of the same species. This may happen by wind or by insect.
   (b) **Fertilisation** is the union of the male and female gamete to produce a fertilised cell (zygote). After fertilisation the ovary is called a fruit.
   (c) **Dispersal** is the scattering of the fruit or individual seeds. This may occur by:
      (i) **Wind:** e.g. dandelion, or winged fruits, e.g. sycamore.
      (ii) **Animal:** the seeds may stick to an animal and be carried some distance, or the animal may eat the seeds which are undigested and are found in the faeces of the animal.
      (iii) Some seeds are **self dispersed** by the plant. The seed pods shrivel in the sun and pop, scatter the seeds, e.g. peas, lupins.
   (d) **Germination:** given favourable conditions the seeds will grow to form new plants. The conditions necessary for germination are:
      (i) heat
      (ii) water
      (iii) oxygen
      (*Note: no light is necessary until the plant produces green leaves.*)

6. **Features of wind pollinated flowers**
   (a) Small inconspicuous flowers with no smell which do not produce nectar.
   (b) Small light pollen grains which do not stick together.
   (c) Large stigmas to aid pollination.

   Features of insect pollinated flowers
   (a) Large flowers with coloured petals, a smell and nectary to attract insects.
   (b) Less pollen is produced.
   (c) Smaller stigmas inside the flower.

Questions

Introduction

1. Plants exhibit the seven characteristics of life. What are they?

2. What role do plants play in the following activities:
   (a) agriculture
   (b) commerce
   (c) leisure activities?

(H) 3. Name two plants which are a source of drugs used in medicine. Also name the drugs produced.

4. Plants are generally composed of a flower, stem, leaves and a root. Give two functions of each of the parts named above.

5. Name two structures found in a typical plant cell that are not found in an animal cell.

6. What is the function of the following parts of a plant cell:
   (a) cell wall
   (b) vacuole
   (c) nucleus
   (d) cell membrane
   (e) chloroplast?

(H) 7. What role do the following structures play in plants:
   (a) phloem
   (b) xylem
   (c) cambium?

Nutrition/Respiration

1. What do you understand by the term photosynthesis?

2. Name the raw materials used by the plant and the products produced by the plant during photosynthesis.

3. What is the word equation for photosynthesis?

(H) 4. Write the chemical equation for photosynthesis.

5. From where does the plant get the energy for photosynthesis, and how is this energy trapped by the plant?

6. Describe an experiment to show that photosynthesis has taken place in a plant.
   Why must the leaves be destarched first?
   How would you remove chlorophyll from the leaf?
   Why is this done?
   What chemical is used to test for starch, and say what colour change you would expect to see if starch were present?

7. How would you show that:
    (a) light
    (b) carbon dioxide
    (c) chlorophyll, were necessary for photosynthesis to take place?

8. How would you demonstrate that a gas was produced during photosynthesis? How would you show that this gas was oxygen?

(H) 9. Name three minerals that a plant needs for healthy growth.
    From where does the plant obtain these minerals?
    How would you show that a deficiency of these minerals inhibits plant growth?

10. What is meant by respiration in plants?
    What gas is:
    (a) taken in
    (b) released during respiration?
    Does respiration occur 24 hours per day?
(H) Write the chemical equation for respiration.

Transport
1. Why do plants need a transport system?

2. Name two materials which are transported from the root of a plant to the leaves.

3. Name one substance which is transported from the leaves to the root of a plant.

(H) 4. What structure transports the materials mentioned in Q.2 and Q.3?

(H) 5. What is meant by transpiration?

(H) 6. How would you show in the laboratory that transpiration occurs in plants?

(H) 7. What weather conditions:
    (a) increase
    (b) decrease the rate of transpiration?

(H) 8. What are the stoma and what function do they play in transpiration?

Tropisms
1. What is a:
    (a) stimulus
    (b) tropism?

2. What is meant by a:
    (a) positive tropism
    (b) negative tropism?
    Give an example in each case.

3. What is phototropism?
   How would you demonstrate phototropism in the laboratory?

H 4. What is geotropism? Describe an experiment to demonstrate geotropism.

5. List two differences in the response of animals and plants to stimuli.

Reproduction
1. What is:
   (a) asexual
   (b) sexual reproduction?

2. Give two advantages of each type of reproduction.

3. What is the organ of reproduction in the plant?

4. Give the function of the following parts of the flower:
   (a) sepal
   (b) petal
   (c) carpel
   (d) stamen.

5. What is the:
   (a) female
   (b) male part of the flower called?

H 6. The female part of the flower has three components. What are they and give one function of each part?

H 7. The male part of the flower has two components. What are they and give one function of each part?

H 8. What is pollination?

H 9. Pollination may occur by wind or insect. List three differences between an insect and a wind pollinated flower.

H 10. How does fertilisation occur in plants?
   What is a fertilised cell called?
   What is a:
   (a) seed
   (b) fruit?

11. What is meant by dispersal of seeds?
    Why is this important?
    Name four methods of seed dispersal and give one feature of the seed that makes that particular method of dispersal suitable.

12. What is germination?
    Name the conditions necessary for germination.
    Why is light not necessary for germination to occur?

(H) 13. Outline and draw a diagram to describe the life cycle of a named plant.

Ecology

Key Points

1. A **habitat** is a place where plants and animals live. There are many different types of habitat, e.g. a pond, a seashore, a hedge, a field.

2. **Animals** and **plants** can be **specific** to **certain habitats**, e.g. crabs may be found in a seashore habitat.

3. There is a need for conservation in a number of habitats, e.g. bogland. **Conservation** is an attempt to preserve animals and plants from extinction.

4. Living things depend on one another for food, shelter, etc. This is called **interrelationships**.

5. **Pollution** is where the environment is damaged by such things as effluent, waste materials, slurry leaking into lakes and rivers, etc.

Habitat study

Key Points

1. **Collecting animals:**
   A **pit fall trap** is used to collect small animals, e.g. insects, beetles.
   Fig. 3.24

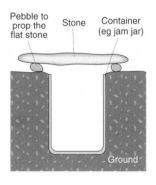

Fig. 3.24

A **pooter** collects small animals by suction.
Fig. 3.25

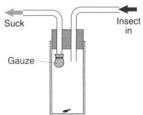

Fig. 3.25

A **sweep net** collects insects.
A **butterfly net** collects butterflies.
A **mammal trap** collects small mammals, e.g. mice.
(*Note: animals should replaced in their habitat unharmed.*)

2. **Plants**
   The distribution of plants is found using a **transect line**.

   Fig. 3.26

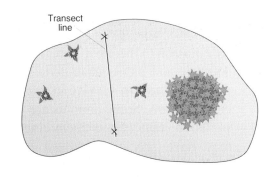

This is a piece of string which is laid across the habitat. The type of vegetation that touches the line is noted. The combination of several transect lines should give a good picture of the type of vegetation in the habitat.

Fig. 3.26

A **quadrat** may also be used to sample the vegetation in a habitat.

Fig. 3.27

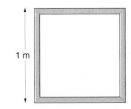

This consists of four pieces of timber joined together to form one metre squares. The quadrat is thrown at random and the type of vegetation inside the quadrat is noted.
The **DAFOR** scale is used to determine the frequency of each species. This stands for **D**ominant, **A**bundant, **F**requent, **O**ccasional and **R**are.

Fig. 3.27

3. **Food Chains**
   Food chains always start with a producer, i.e. a plant. The next level is a **primary consumer** which eats plants, i.e. a herbivore. The next level is an **animal** that eats other animals, i.e. a carnivore, which is a secondary consumer.

   e.g.   Grass   →   Rabbit   →   Fox

 4. **Trophic levels**
   The primary producers are a solar energy trap, making organic material for the next level, i.e. the herbivores or primary consumers. These in turn provide food for the next level, the carnivores or secondary consumers. These levels are known as trophic levels.

H **5. Food webs**

A food web gives a more accurate account of the feeding patterns in a habitat. It consists of a series of food chains which are interlinked.
Fig. 3.28

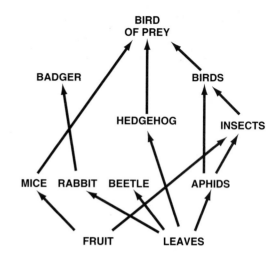

Fig. 3.28

6. Adaptation to the environment.

Animals and plants have certain features that allow them **to survive in a particular environment**. Some animals are coloured so as to camouflage themselves. Birds may have specially adapted beaks for feeding. Some water birds have webbed feet for swimming, e.g. swans. A hawk has good eyesight for hunting.

7. Competition

Plants compete with one another for light, water and space. This occurs within the same species and between different species.

Animals compete for food (within the same species and between species) and mates (within the same species).

8. Interdependence

This is where animals and plants are dependent on one another, e.g. plants are dependent on animals (insects) for pollination and animals (bees) are dependent on plants for food (nectar).

Soil Study

Key Points

1. **Soil** consists of gravel, stones, silt, clay and humus. These particles can be seen if a sample of soil is placed in a graduated cylinder. The graduated cylinder is then filled with water and shaken. When it has settled the different components of soil are visible in layers.
Fig. 3.29

Soil contains water with dissolved minerals and also air spaces. Many organisms live in the soil, e.g. the earthworm.

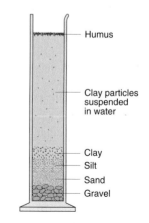

Fig. 3.29

2. It is possible, by experiment, to determine the percentage of **water**, the percentage of **humus** and the percentage of **air** in a soil sample. The pH of a soil sample can also be found. A **Tullgren funnel** is capable of extracting small organisms from the soil.

Questions

1. What is conservation? List two consequences of not conserving nature.

2. What do you understand by pollution?
   Name two sources of pollution.
   How can pollution be controlled?

(H) 3. How is deforestation caused?
   Is there any way of stopping this problem?
   List two effects of deforestation.

(H) 4. How does desertification arise?
   How can this be prevented?

5. What is a habitat? Give an example of a habitat from your local area that you have studied.

6. Describe how you would make a map of a habitat that you have studied?

7. List three plants and three animals from the habitat.

8. Describe with the aid of a diagram how you would use:
   (a) a pooter
   (b) a pitfall trap.
   Name two other methods of collecting small animals that are available to you.

9. Name two methods by which you can estimate the vegetation in a habitat.

10. What is the DAFOR scale?

11. From your habitat, give an example of:
    (a) interdependence
    (b) competition between species
    (c) competition between the same species
    (d) adaptation.

12. What is a primary producer? Give an example.

13. What is a consumer? Give an example.

14. Construct two food chains from the habitat that you have studied. What is always the first link of the chain?

(H) 15. What is the difference between a food web and a food chain? Give an example of a food web from a habitat you have studied.
    Which is the most accurate representation of what occurs in a habitat? Explain.

(H) 16. What do you understand by trophic level?
At what level(s) would you find consumers?

(H) 17. Give four reasons why it is necessary to have a good policy for the management of the earth's resources?

18. What is humus? How would you find the percentage of humus in a soil sample?

19. How would you find the pH of a soil sample?

20. Describe how you would find the percentage of water in a soil sample. In such an experiment 9 gms of soil was weighed and at the end of the experiment it was weighed again and found to be 6.5 gms. What was the percentage of water in the sample?

21. How would you demonstrate that soil consists of many different types of material: sand, clay, humus, gravel, etc.?

22. How would you show that there are air spaces in soil?

23. Name an organism that you would expect to find in soil.

24. For what would you use a Tullgren funnel?
Describe, using a labelled diagram, how you would use such an instrument.

(H) 25. Name three minerals that you would expect to find in a sample of soil.

26. What is meant by leaching?
What is the disadvantage of leaching?

(H) 27. How would you demonstrate that there are micro-organisms present in soil?

Chapter 4   APPLIED SCIENCE

Earth Science

Key Points

1. The **universe** consists of space and a collection of galaxies.

2. **Galaxies** consist of a series of solar systems and stars.
    Our galaxy is called the **Milky Way**.

3. A **solar system** consists of a sun, planets and moons.

4. The **earth** is the only planet known to be capable of supporting life as we know it – the reasons for this are:
    (a) it is neither too hot or too cold
    (b) it has water
    (c) it has oxygen.

5. The **sun is a star**. The energy of the sun comes from the fusion reaction of two hydrogen atoms forming helium.

6. A **year** is the time it takes the earth to orbit the sun.

7. A **day** is the time it takes the earth to rotate once on its axis.

8. The earth is tilted at 23° to the vertical. When the northern hemisphere is tilted towards the sun, it has summer and when it is tilted away from the sun it has winter.
    Fig. 4.1

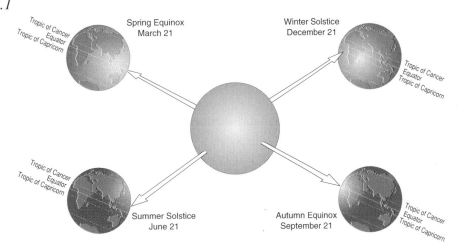

Fig. 4.1

9. A **solar eclipse** occurs when the moon comes between the earth and the sun, blocking out the sun's rays. It is seen during the day.
    Fig. 4.2

10. A **lunar eclipse** occurs when the earth comes between the sun and the moon, blocking the sunlight getting to the moon. It is seen at night.
    Fig. 4.3

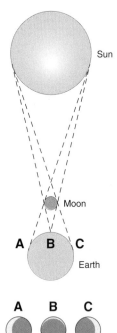

View from Earth of the Sun

Fig. 4.2

Fig. 4.3

H   Life cycle of a star.

1. **Formation:** dust particles and hydrogen are gathered by gravitational forces. The gravitational energy is converted to heat energy and enable fusion reactions to occur.

2. **Stable State:** fusion reactions occur for millions of years. Our sun is in its stable state.

3. **Red Giant:** the sun becomes red and increases in size.

4. **White Dwarf:** the fuel runs out and the star shrinks in size and it is called a white dwarf.

The Moon

Key Points

1. The moon is a **satellite** of the earth because it orbits the earth.

2. The moon is not luminous but it **reflects** sunlight. Depending on the relative position of the moon and the earth, different parts of the moon are illuminated and this is known as the phases of the moon.
   Fig. 4.4

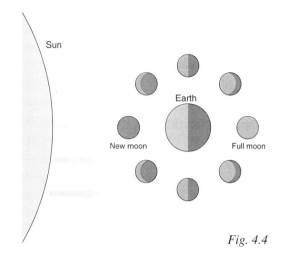

Fig. 4.4

(H) 3. **Tides** are caused by the gravitational pull of the sun and the moon.

(H) 4. The effect of the moon on the tides is greater because the moon is nearer to the earth.

(H) 5. **Spring tides** occur when the moon and the sun are pulling in the direction illustrated in *Fig. 4.5*

(H) 6. **Neap tides** occur when the gravitational forces of the moon and the sun are perpendicular to each other.
   Fig. 4.6

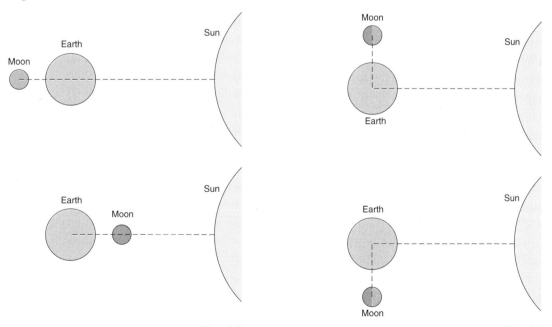

Fig. 4.5

Fig. 4.6

7. In our solar system, nine planets orbit the sun.
    From the sun, they are Mercury, Venus, Earth, Mars, Jupiter, Saturn, Uranus, Neptune, Pluto.

H 8. Students are required to compare one planet and the moon with the earth.

	Earth	**Moon**	**Venus**
Diameter (Km)	12,756	3,476	12,180
Distance from Sun (Km)	152,000,000		108,230,000
Surface Gravity	1	0.17	0.88
Surface Temperature (Celcius)	–60 to +60	–60	480
Atmosphere	nitrogen, oxygen, carbon dioxide, water vapour	none	carbon dioxide, nitrogen, argon, water vapour
Moons	1	–	none

Water in the atmosphere

Key Points

1. **Evaporation and condensation** are dependent on temperature and on wind. The former occurs most efficiently in warm windy conditions and the latter occurs in cool calm conditions.

2. **Humidity** is the amount of water vapour in the atmosphere. Relative humidity is measured using a **hygrometer**.

H 3. **Cloud** occurs when water vapour in the air rises, it cools and forms tiny droplets. These droplets come together to form clouds. The main types of cloud are cirrus, stratus and cumulus.

H 4. **Fog** is a cloud at ground level, i.e. water vapour at ground level.

H 5. **Frost** occurs when the temperature drops below 0°C. Then water vapour in the air forms ice. This is frost.

Pressure in the atmosphere

Key Points

1. **Atmospheric pressure** is measured using an **Aneroid Barometer**. As we ascend the density of the atmosphere decreases. The pressure also decreases so that on the top of a mountain the atmospheric pressure is less than at sea level.

2. **Boyles' Law:** The pressure of a given mass of gas is inversely proportional to its volume, if the temperature is constant.
$$P_1 X V_1 = P_2 X V_2$$

(H) 3. **Charles' Law:** The volume of a given mass of gas is directly proportional to the absolute (Kelvin) temperature, if the pressure is constant.
$$V_1/T_1 = V_2/T_2$$

4. Energy is transferred from the sun to the earth by radiation. Some of this energy is absorbed by the atmosphere, some by the earth, some by plants and the remaining energy is reflected back into space.
   The increasing level of **carbon dioxide** in the atmosphere is causing concern as it prevents the reflection of heat from the earth back to space, thereby causing global warming. This is known as the **greenhouse effect**, one of its consequences is the melting of the polar ice caps, leading to rising sea levels. Increased carbon dioxide levels are due to an increased use of fossil fuels in industry and in cars.

5. **Onshore breezes**
   During the day, land heats up more quickly the the sea. The hot air rises and cool air from over the sea blows in to replace it, causing an onshore breeze.
   Fig. 4.7

6. **Offshore breezes**
   At night, the sea retains its heat longer than land. The warm air over the sea rises and the result is an offshore breeze.
   Fig. 4.8

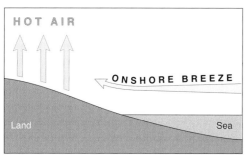

HOT AIR

ONSHORE BREEZE

Land   Sea

Fig. 4.7

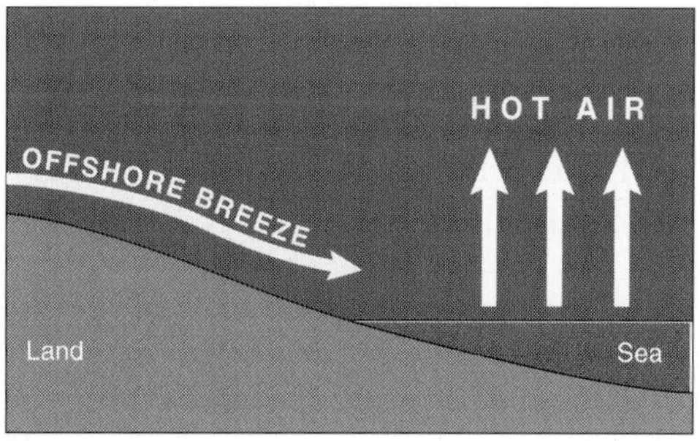

OFFSHORE BREEZE

HOT AIR

Land   Sea

Fig. 4.8

Recording the weather

Key Points

1. **Wind speed** is measured using an **anemometer** and wind direction is measured using a **weather vane**.

2. **Atmospheric pressure** is measured using a barometer.

3. **Temperature** is measured using a **thermometer**, which is kept out of direct sunlight in a **Stevenson Screen**. A maximum/minimum thermometer records the highest and the lowest temperature in a day or any other period of time.

4. **Rainfall** can be measured using a **rain gauge** and a **graduated cylinder**.

Questions

1. What is the universe?

2. What is a galaxy? What galaxy do we live in?

3. What is meant by a solar system?

4. Name the fourth and the ninth planets from the sun?

5. Give three reasons why the earth is able to sustain life.

6. Why do the other planets in the solar system not support life as we know it?

H 7. List the four stages in the life cycle of a star.
   Which stage is our sun in?
   What type of reaction occurs in the sun?
   Why does a star become faint and eventually die?

8. What is meant by a:
   (a) day
   (b) a year, in terms of the movement of the earth?

9. What is an eclipse?
   Illustrate by diagrams:
   (a) a lunar eclipse
   (b) a solar eclipse.

   What type of eclipse would you observe during the:
   (a) day
   (b) night?

10. Show, by diagram, the origin of the seasons.

11. What is a moon? Is the moon luminous? What is meant by the phases of the moon?

H 12. How do you account for the origin of tides?
What is meant by:
(a) a spring tide
(b) a neap tide?
Illustrate by a diagram how they occur.

H 13. Compare the earth with a named planet under the headings:
(a) Relative size
(b) Distance from the sun
(c) Gravity
(d) Atmosphere
(e) Number of moons

14. Explain the following terms: evaporation, condensation, humidity.
What is the difference between evaporation and boiling?
How would you measure humidity?

15. How would you show that there is water in the atmosphere?
H How are clouds formed?
H Outline an experiment to show the formation of a cloud.

H 16. What is:
(a) fog
(b) frost?

17. How would you show that the atmosphere exerts pressure?
How would you measure atmospheric pressure?
How does atmospheric pressure vary as we ascend?
What instrument is based on this phenomena?

H 18. State Boyles' Law.
Describe an experiment to demonstrate Boyles' Law.

H 19. The pressure of 500cm³ of gas is 1500 Pascals. What would the volume be at 2000 Pascals, if the temperature remains constant?

H 20. 600cm³ of gas is placed in a sealed container, the pressure of which is 2000 Pa. What would be the pressure of 800cm³ of the same gas under similar conditions?

H 21. State Charles' Law.
Describe an experiment to demonstrate Charles' Law.

H 22. The volume of a gas is 1000cm³ at a temperature of 300° Kelvin. What would the volume be at
(a)   500°
(b)   200° Kelvin, if the pressure does not change?

H 23. How is the sun's energy transferred to earth?

H 24. What is meant by the term 'greenhouse effect'?
What are the consequences of the greenhouse effect for us on earth?
What measures can we take to curtail this effect?

H 25. Illustrate by means of a diagram how the following occur:
(a)   onshore breeze
(b)   offshore breeze.
What is the effect of these breezes on the temperature of a coastal region?

26. List four measurements that you would take to record the weather.
What piece of apparatus would you use for each measurement?
Draw a labelled diagram of each piece of apparatus.
How would you take one of these measurements over a period of time?
Why would you do this?
What type of weather would you expect in Ireland during the winter with:
(a)   high pressure
(b)   low pressure?

Horticulture

Key Points

1. **Soil, Compost, Plant Nutrition**
   Plants need a **growing medium**. Such media include **soil**, **compost** and **water**.
   Soil consists of gravel, sand, silt, clay, humus, water, air and minerals.
   Compost is a growing medium of soil, peat and sand, or it is a substance produced from rotting garden waste which can be used as a mulch or as a fertiliser.
   Hydroponics is growing plants in water to which minerals have been added. A substance may be added to anchor plants, e.g. vermiculite.
   Earthworms create air spaces in soil, they break up the soil and they add humus to the soil.
   Plant nutrients: nitrogen, phosphorus and potassium are essential minerals for plant growth.

2. **Seeds and cuttings**
   Seeds do not germinate immediately but go through a period of dormancy. This stops the seeds germinating during the winter.
   In order to **germinate** seeds need **oxygen**, **heat** and **water**.

Taking a **cutting** involves cutting a piece of stem and leaves, encouraging a root to develop and planting the cutting. A plant identical to the original plant develops.

Hard wood cuttings are taken from plants with woody stems and they are planted outside.

Soft wood cuttings are removed from the tips of plants when they are growing, a root is encouraged and the cutting is planted.

3. **Growing practices**

   In order to achieve optimum plant growth, several factors are necessary.

   (a)   Availability of **water**.
   (b)   **Oxygen** is needed for respiration and **carbon dioxide** for photosynthesis.
   (c)   A suitable **temperature** – some plants require heat, others prefer cooler conditions.
   (d)   **Space** in which to grow.
   (e)   **Minerals**, e.g. nitrates, phosphates and potassium.

Grasses

Bent has fine leaves and is used on the greens of golf courses.

Fescue has fine leaves and tolerates a lot of cutting. It is suitable for grazing.

Dwarf ryegrass is a tough grass and is used for sports grounds and also for grazing.

Naturalised meadow is where the grass is allowed to grow to maturity and it is a habitat for many animals.

A **mulch** is a layer consisting of bark chippings, gravel, compost or black plastic. This prevents the soil from dying out and it helps to control weeds.

Aftercare of cut flowers:

   (a)   they need an adequate supply of water. The water needs to be changed regularly.
   (b)   dipping the stems in bleach will kill bacteria.

4. **Diseases and pests:**

   Crop protection: the life cycle of the white cabbage butterfly *(Fig. 4.9)* **or** the aphid *(Fig. 4.10)* to be known by the student.

   The host plant of the cabbage white butterfly is the cabbage.

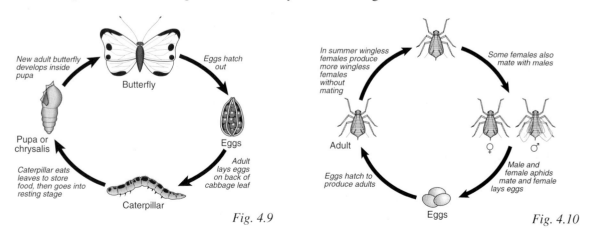

Fig. 4.9

Fig. 4.10

Pest control: a pest is an organism that competes with humans for food.

Biological control: birds eat caterpillars, limiting the number of butterflies that develop.

Chemical control: plants are sprayed with chemicals which kill pests.

Integrated pest control: where possible natural methods of pest control are used and only when these fail should chemical methods be used.

Questions

1. What growing media are available for growing plants?

2. Explain what is meant by hydroponics.

3. What are the components of soil?

4. What is compost? What is compost used for?

5. How would you measure the percentage of water and the percentage of air in a soil sample?

6. What role do earthworms play in the soil?

(H) 7. How would you measure the pH of a soil sample?

(H) 8. List three elements necessary for the healthy growth of plants. Describe an experiment to show how the lack of these elements affects plant growth.

9. What is meant by the saying that a seed is dormant? What is the reason for a period of dormancy in plants?

10. Describe how you would grow a named plant from a seed.

11. What is a cutting? Why are cuttings taken rather than sowing seeds?

(H) 12. What is grafting? In your answer explain what is a scion and what is a stock? What type of plants are suitable for grafting? What is the advantage of grafting?

13. What is photosynthesis? What raw materials does the plant need for photosynthesis and where does the plant get these raw materials from?

(H) 14. For what purpose is:
    (a) bent
    (b) fiscue
    (c) dwarf ryegrass used?
    What is a naturalised meadowland?

15. How would you care for a named bedding plant?

(H) 16. What is a mulch? For what purposes are mulches used?

17. How would you care for cut flowers?

18. Outline the life cycle of the cabbage white butterfly or aphid. What is the host plant of the pest? How would you control the pest?

(H) 19. What is meant by biological pest control? What do you understand by chemical pest control? What are the advantages and disadvantages of each method?

(H) 20. Name a pest found in the garden. How would you control it?

21. What is:
    (a) an annual plant, (b) a biennial plant and (c) a perennial plant?

22. What is meant by vegetative plant propagation?

23. How would you determine the percentage germination of a sample of seeds?

24. What are the advantages of growing seeds in a greenhouse?

25. Describe how you would grow a potted plant under the following headings:
    (a) growing medium used.
    (b) propagation.
    (c) watering. How would you ensure that the plant was watered if you were on holiday?

26. You have been asked to plant a flower bed with spring flowers outline the steps that you would take.

Materials

Key Points

1. **Materials** may be classified as **natural or synthetic** (man-made). Timber is an example of a natural material, while nylon is a synthetic material.
   There are many categories of material, e.g.

Material	Example
hydrocarbon	natural gas
textile	terylene
plastic	PVC
metal	copper

2. Materials may be mixed to give improved properties. An **alloy** is generally a mixture of two metals, e.g. brass is made from copper and zinc. Fabrics may be mixed to improve their properties, e.g. polyester/cotton.

3. The same material may have different uses, e.g. plastics may be used in window frames, car construction and pens.

4. **Care of materials:**
    Metals corrode and can be protected by paint, grease, oil, galvanising, electroplating, etc.
    Timber can rot or be attacked by various insects or fungi. It can be **protected** by paint, polish and preservatives.
    Plastics can be affected by heat, sunlight, etc., and these should be avoided.
    Textiles can be damaged by fire, heat, insects and incorrect washing.
    The manufacturer's instructions and labels should be followed to care adequately for materials.
    Students taking the Lower Course should study one of the following sections and those taking the Higher Course should study two of the following sections.

    Metals
    An **ore** is a metal which is found mixed with other materials. There are two stages in the extraction of a metal. The ore is separated from the rest of the rock and the metal is extracted from the ore by **smelting**.
    Some metals are found free in nature, e.g. gold.
    Metals are:
    Malleable: they can be hammered into sheets.
    Ductile: they can be made into wires.
    Good conductors of heat and electricity.
    Lustre: they are shiny.

    Textiles
    Fabrics are made up of strands of **yarn** which in turn are made up of **fibres**.
    Fabrics can be **natural or synthetic** (man-made), natural fabrics can be of **animal** or **vegetable** origin.

Material	Origin
fur	animal
cotton	plant
terylene	synthetic

    Plastics
    Plastics are **polymers** made up from small molecules called **monomers** which are derived from **oil**.
    Thermoplastics can be remoulded, they consist of long chained polymers without cross links.

Thermosetting plastics are long chained polymers with cross links. They cannot be remoulded. Plastics have many uses which depend on their hardness, flexibility, density, flammability, and insulating properties. They can be dangerous when burned because they can produce toxic fumes.

Timber

Timber coming from trees is a **natural** material.

Hardwood comes from broad-leafed trees, e.g. oak. It takes a long time to mature and it is used in boat building and in making furniture.

Softwoods come from trees with narrow needle like leafs, e.g. fir trees, spruce. They are used for making paper and for making pallets and floors.

Advantages of forestry

(a) It provides employment.
(b) It is a renewable source of material.
(c) It provides a habitat for plants and animals.
(d) The products can be exported and imports may be reduced.
(e) Trees can grow on land which may not be suitable for farming.

Green timber comes directly from the tree and may contain a lot of water.
Oven dried timber contains less water.

Processed timber

Plywood: sheets of timber are glued together with the grains at right angles to one another. It comes in a variety of thicknesses and it can be used to make cheap furniture.

Chipboard: this is made from chippings of timber glued together and compressed into sheets. It is used in flooring.

Blockboard: made from strips of wood which are glued together and covered with a veneer.

A **veneer** is a thin sheet of wood, used to cover other timber. It is used in furniture making.

Hardboard: waste timber is crushed to form wood fibre. It is treated with chemicals to harden it and it is compressed. One surface has a smooth surface and the other side is rough. It is used for panelling.

Questions

A   **Identification of Materials**

1. What is the difference between a natural and a man-made material? Give an example of each.

2. Give an example of one material in each case from the following categories:
   Hydrocarbon   Plastic   Textile   Metal

3. Materials may be mixed to give improved properties. In the case of a named textile, name the materials present and give one improved property.

4. What is an alloy? Give two examples of alloys. In the case of both examples state what each alloy is made of and give a use to which each may be put.

5. Steel is an alloy consisting of a mixture of a metal and a non-metal. Name both components of steel and give three uses of steel.

B   Use of materials

6. It is possible to use different materials for the same purpose. Name three materials from which a kitchen spoon may be made. Name two other items that can be made from different materials and say what these materials are.

7. The same material can be put to different uses. In the case of a named
   (a) metal   (b) textile   (c) plastic,
   list three uses to which each may be put.

8. How would you protect timber from
   (a)   the weather
   (b)   rotting due to fungus
   (c)   woodworm?

9. Textiles require special care. Identify the following symbols that may be found on different clothes. *Fig. 4.11*

Fig. 4.11

10. What happens when iron is exposed to the weather? Give four methods of protection from the weather.

11. What is meant by the term biodegradable? Are:
    (a) plastics
    (b) timber, biodegradable?
    Explain.

12. Name two things that can damage plastics. How can damage to plastics be prevented?

13. From the following list of items, classify them according to the categories metal, textile or plastic:

fibreglass, silk, terylene, bronze, polythene, aluminium, formica, wool, copper.

14. If you were designing a sofa, list four properties that the upholstery would need to have.

Ordinary level students need to cover one section and Higher level students need to cover two sections from C, D, E, F.

C Plastics

1. Where do plastics come from? Is this a renewable or a non-renewable supply? Explain.

2. What is a:
   (a) monomer   (b) polymer?

3. Give one use of the following plastics:
   (a) Polythene   (b) Polyvinylchloride (PVC)
   (c) Polystyrene   (d) Nylon
   (e) Perspex.

4. How would you compare the:
   (a) flexibility   (b) hardness of plastics?

5. How would you find the density of plastic in the laboratory?

6. What are the problems associated with burning plastics?

D Textiles

1. What is meant by the following terms: textile, fabric, yarn, fibre?

2. Give three examples each of
   (a) a natural fibre   (b) a man-made fibre.

3. Give two examples each of a fabric that is of
   (a) plant   (b) animal
   (c) man-made origin.

4. What is the origin of man-made fibres?

5. Why are fabrics mixed, e.g. polyester/cotton, terylene/wool?

6. List five properties of a fabric that need to be considered when using that fabric to make clothes.

7. How would you compare the insulating properties of two textiles, e.g. cotton and wool?

8. What is meant by the term absorbancy? How would you compare the absorbancy of cotton, nylon and wool?

9. Describe an apparatus to compare the resistance to wear of two textiles. How would you use such an apparatus to compare the resistance to wear of nylon, cotton and wool?

10. What is meant by the term flammability of textiles? List two problems that are associated with burning textiles. How may these problems be prevented?

11. What properties should the following materials have? Name a suitable textile in each case:
    (a) a vest
    (b) a raincoat
    (c) a sail for a yacht
    (d) a tent
    (e) a curtain.

12. Is the following use of textiles good or bad? Support your answer with a reason.
    (a) a nylon vest
    (b) cotton clothes for mountaineering
    (c) a terylene sail
    (d) woollen cushion covers
    (e) a cotton raincoat.

E   **Metals**
 1. What is a metal ore?

 2. Name one ore of copper. Describe an experiment to extract this ore from the ground.

 3. Name two mines in Ireland that are still in existence. What metals are mined in these mines?

 4. List four uses of metals by people during the Bronze Age in Ireland. What use do we make of metals in Ireland today?

 5. How would you compare the hardness of iron, steel and copper?

 6. How would you compare the flexibility of metals?

 7. Describe an experiment to determine which of four metals is the best conductor of heat.

 8. How would you find the density of a metal? Name and give a use for a:
     (a) high density metal
     (b) low density metal.

 9. Name the only metal which is a liquid at room temperature. Give one use of this metal.

10. What do you understand by the electrochemical series?
     Place the following metals in increasing order of reactivity:
     gold, copper, sodium, zinc, aluminium.

11. Why do you think that gold was known to the ancient people of Ireland, and aluminium was only isolated recently?

12. What do the following terms mean: malleable, ductile, lustre, smelting, metal fatigue?

13. How would you show that metals conduct electricity and non-metals generally do not conduct electricity?

F   **Timber and constructed boards**

1. What is the origin of timber?

2. What is meant by man-made boards? Why have these been developed?

3. List five advantages of the development of forestry in Ireland.

4. What is
   (a) a hardwood   (b) a softwood?
   Give two examples of each type.

5. What is meant by the term 'greenwood'? How is this wood processed?

6. Give three advantages of using constructed boards. Plywood, blockboard, chipboard and hardboard are all constructed boards. How are each made and mention one use of each?

7. How, in the laboratory, would you compare the strength of different types of timber? Is the thickness of each important? Why?

8. How would you find the density of a piece of timber?

9. When plywood is manufactured, the grains of adjacent layers are at right angles to one another. What is the reason for this?

10. Is timber a renewable or a non-renewable resource? Explain.

11. Over 85% of forestry in Ireland is devoted to growing soft woods. What is the reason for this?

12. From the following list, oak, spruce, plywood, teak, scot's pine, hardboard, identify:
   (a) the hard woods   (b) the soft woods
   (c) the man-made boards.

   From which material in the list would you make:
   (a) a bureau   (b) a garden shed
   (c) a boat   (d) a floor for the attic?
   Explain your answer.

13. What is a veneer? Give two advantages of using a veneer.

H 14. Most materials deteriorate for a number of reasons: weather, pest infection, corrosion, etc. Give two reasons for the deterioration of the following and say how each can be protected from this deterioration:
   (a) a garden seat made out of oak   (b) a garden gate made out of iron
   (c) a garden shed made out of plywood   (d) a metal fork
   (e) Plastic bumpers on a car.

15. What are the following symbols used for?
    Fig. 4.12

Fig. 4.12

Food

Key Points

1. There are **seven constituents in the diet**: carbohydrates, fats, proteins, vitamins, minerals, water, fibre.
   A **balanced diet** consists of the correct amount of the different types of food.

Food Type	Source	Function	Elements present
carbohydrates	bread, pasta, potatoes, rice	source of energy	carbon, oxygen, hydrogen,
proteins	dairy products, eggs, meat, fish	growth and repair	carbon, oxygen, nitrogen hydrogen,
fats	butter, oils, fatty meat	insulation, energy	carbon, oxygen, hydrogen

Food type	Test
starch	Drop iodine solution on to the food to be tested. If a blue-black colour appears, starch is present.
reducing sugar	Add Benedicts solution to a sample of the food. Heat. If a colour change occurs, a reducing sugar is present. (Note, Fehlings solution may also be used.)
proteins	Biuret test: add sodium hydroxide to a sample of the food. Add a few drops of copper sulphate solution. A violet colour indicates the presence of a protein.
fat	Smear the food on to a piece of brown paper. Heat the paper gently and hold up to the light. A translucent spot appears if fat is present.

Vitamins are used by the body to prevent disease and to assist with the growth process. (Know any two).

Vitamin	Source	Deficiency disease
A	milk, butter, carrots and other vegetables	night blindness
B group	yeast, meat, unpolished cereal grain	Beriberi
C	citrus fruits, tomatoes	scurvy
D	fish liver oils, butter	Rickets

Minerals are required by the body in small amounts. (Know any two).

Mineral	Source	Use
iron	egg yolk, liver, cabbage	to make haemoglobin
calcium	milk, cheese	helps to strengthen bones
iodine	sea salt	needed for the thyroid gland
phosphorus	yoghurt	bone formation

2. **Food Additives**

These are chemicals added to food to:
(a)   preserve the food
(b)   colour the food
(c)   flavour the food

Additives are coded
E: the additive is permitted by the EU.
The first number tells us the type of additive:

Number	Function
1	colouring
2	preservative
3	anti-oxidants
4	stabilisers and emulsifiers

Advantages of food additives:
(a)   food looks better.
(b)   food has a longer shelf life.
(c)   food tastes better.

Disadvantages of food additives:
(a) Some additives are **unhealthy**.
(b) **Hormones** used as growth promoters in farm animals and antibiotics may remain in animal produce and get into human systems.
(c) Some additives may cause **allergic reactions**.

3. **Food preservation**
Some micro-organisms cause food to go bad. Various methods of food preservation are used to stop this happening.

Method	Food
pasteurisation	milk
canning	fruit, soup, vegetables
dehydration	soup, milk , fruit
curing	bacon
smoking	fish , meat
placing in syrup solution	fruit
irradiation	meat (especially pork)
pickling	onions , beetroot
salting	bacon

freezing   meat, veg, fruit

4. **The food industry**
The dairy industry uses **milk** to manufacture a variety of products including: cheese, yoghurt, butter and milk products.
Pasteurisation occurs when milk is heated to just below its boiling point in order to **kill bacteria** which are present. The milk is then cooled quickly to retain its flavour.
Silage is made by the action of bacteria on the food in grass and is used as a method of preserving grass for feeding animals.
Biotechnology is the use of living organisms in research and in industrial processes.
Fermentation occurs when organisms are respiring **anaerobically** and producing alcohol or lactic acid.

5. **World food supply**
Food is not equally distributed among people. The richer Western World **over-produces** food while the poorer Third World **under-produces** food.
The cause of under-production of food may be **low rainfall**, which results in drought or **inadequate farming methods**. The result may be **illness, malnutrition** (where people do not have a balanced diet) or **starvation**.

Questions

1. Why do we eat?
   List the seven constituents of the diet.

2. Name three foods which are a good source of carbohydrates.
   For what purpose does the body use carbohydrates?
   What are carbohydrates broken down to in the body?
   How would you test a food sample for starch?
   Name a food that would give a positive result for such a test.

3. Reducing sugars can be identified by using Fehlings solution.
   Describe how you would use Fehlings solution to test a sample of food for reducing sugars.
   What colour change would you expect to observe?
   What other solution could you use to test for sugar?

4. What is the function of protein in the diet?
   Name three foods that are rich in protein.
   How would you test a sample of food to show the presence of protein?
   What are proteins broken down to in the body?

5. Name three foods that are rich in fats.
   What is the function of fats in the diet?
   How would you test a sample of food to show the fat is present?
   What are fats broken down to in the body?

6. Why is fibre important in the diet?
   Name two foods which are good sources of fibre.

H 7. List the chemical elements that are present in:
   (a) carbohydrates
   (b) proteins
   (c) fats.

8. Why are minerals important in the diet?
   Name two minerals which are important in the diet. Where do we obtain these minerals from and what function do they have in the body?

H 9. Why are vitamins important in the diet? Name two vitamins and say from which food do we obtain them. Why are the named vitamins important for the body?

10. What is meant by the term 'balanced diet'?

11. Give one:
    (a) advantage
    (b) disadvantage of dieting.

12. From the following list: butter, rice, fish cheese, milk, liver, bread, olive oil, oranges, potatoes, crisps, jam, eggs, pick out two sources of:
    (a) protein   (b) fat
    (c) carbohydrate   (d) starch
    (e) vitamins   (f) calcium (1 source)
    (g) iron (1 source).

13. List three disadvantages of being overweight.

14. List three causes of famine.
    What are the effects of famine?
    In what ways can we help countries whose people suffer from famine?

15. Why do we preserve food?

16. Milk is preserved by pasteurisation. How is milk pasteurised?

17. How would you show that there are micro-organisms present in food?
    In what conditions do micro-organisms thrive?

18. How do the following methods of food preservation work, and name two foods that can be preserved by each method:
    (a) freezing, (b) canning, (c) dehydration, (d) use of chemical additives?

H 19. How does salting work to preserve food?
    Name four types of food that can be preserved by this method.

H 20. Jam can be preserved by using a sugar solution. How does this method work?

H 21. What is meant by irradiation of food?
    What type of food is preserved by this method?

22. How would you preserve the following foods:
    carrots, soup, bacon, salmon, onions, milk, pears?

23. What is a food additive?
    List three advantages and three disadvantages of food additives.

24. Why are colourings added to food?

H 25. Name three types of preservative which are added to food.

H 26. What is the function of anti-oxidants? Name two foods to which these chemicals are added.

27. What is the function of stabilisers and emulsifiers?
    To what types of food are these added?

28. Name two foods to which sweetners are added.

29. What is an E number?
    What does the first number tell you?

30. What is meant by the term food processing?

31. Name four products of the dairy industry.

32. Briefly outline how you would make:
    (a) butter   (b) cheese   (c) yoghurt from milk?

33. What is meant by:
    (a) curing   (b) smoking?
    What type of foods undergo this process?

34. What is fermentation?
    How would you show that carbon dioxide is a product of fermentation?
    What other useful product is obtained in this process?
    What organism is used in fermentation?
    Is the organism respiring aerobically or anaerobically? Explain.
    What industries are dependent on this process?

H 35. What are the advantages and disadvantages of using antibiotics and growth hormones in cattle production?

36. What is silage?
    Why do farmers use silage for growing cattle?
    Outline how you would prepare a sample of silage in the laboratory.

H 37. Define biotechnology. Name two products of biotechnology.

Electronics

Key Points

1. A **diode** is a device which allows current to flow in one direction only.

   A diode has a **forward bias** if the cathode of the diode is connected to the negative terminal of a battery. If the direction of the arrow is the same as the direction of the current, the diode has a forward bias, otherwise it has a reverse bias. This allows current to flow through the diode.

   A diode has a **reverse bias** if the cathode of the diode is connected to the positive terminal of a battery. This will not allow current to flow.
   Fig. 4.13

   A diode can act as a **rectifier** which converts Alternating Current (A.C.) to Direct Current (D.C.)

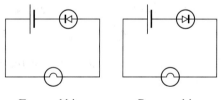

Forward bias   Reverse bias

Fig. 4.13

2. When current flows through a light emitting diode it gives out either red, green or yellow light. For light to be emitted the diode must be connected in the forward bias. It is protected by a resistor in series. *Fig. 4.14*

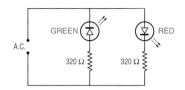

Fig. 4.14

3. A switch makes or breaks a circuit.
Switches in series (Fig. 4.15 (i))
For current to flow through the circuit, both switches must be closed. This is the basis of the **"AND" gate**.

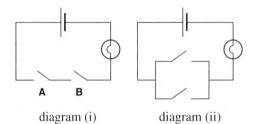

diagram (i)   diagram (ii)   *Fig. 4.15*

Switches in parallel (Fig. 4.15 (ii))
For current to flow through the circuit, either switch must be closed. This is the basis of the **"OR" gate**.

4. A **variable resistor** can be used to vary the current flowing in a circuit. It can also be used as a **potentiometer** to vary the voltage.

5. **Light dependent resistors (LDR's)** are used where the current flowing in a circuit needs to be controlled by the amount of light falling on the resistor. They use the principle that when light falls on the LDR the resistance changes. They are found in burglar alarms and in street lighting.

6. A **transistor** can be used as a switch or as an amplifier.
Fig 4.16
It has three terminals: the base, the collector and the emitter.

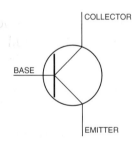

7. A **transducer** is used to convert energy from one form to another, e.g. a photocell converts light energy to electricity.

Fig. 4.16

Questions

1. What is a diode? Will a current flow through a diode in forward bias or a diode in reverse bias?

2. Which bulb will light in *Fig. 4.13*? Why?

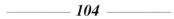

3. What is the difference between Alternating and Direct current?

4. What is a rectifier? Draw a sketch of the output you would expect to see on a cathode ray oscilloscope of half wave rectification. How would you get full wave rectification?

5. Draw a diagram to show:
    (i)   three bulbs in series
    (ii) three bulbs in parallel.

    Where you expect to find bulbs connected in:
    (i)   series
    (ii) parallel?

    What is the disadvantage of connecting bulbs in series?

6. Draw a circuit with two bulbs in parallel, where both bulbs can be switched on or off independently of one another.

7. What is a Light Emitting Diode (L.E.D.)? Draw the symbol for such a device. To what use may L.E.D's be put? How is an L.E.D. protected?

8. Explain what you observe happening in the circuit in *Fig 4.14*. What would happen if the current supply was changed to a direct supply? What is the purpose of the resistor?

9. Draw a circuit that you could use to test the polarity of a battery.

10. What is a switch? How are the switches arranged in *Fig. 4.15*? In diagram (i), do both switches have to be closed in order for the bulb to light? In diagram (ii), how many switches need to be closed for the bulb to light? Which arrangement could be used for an (i) AND gate (ii) OR gate?

11. What is a two way switch? Where are we likely to find such an arrangement? Draw a diagram to illustrate a two way switch, using a battery and a bulb.

H 12. Give a possible application of a water level detector. Draw a circuit to show how such a device works. Could you use the device to determine the level of oil in a central heating tank, or the level of petrol in the tank of a car? Explain your answer.

13. What is a variable resistor? What is another name for this device? Name two places where you would use a variable resistor.

H 14. Give two uses of light dependent resistors.

H 15. What is a thermistor? Give two applications of such a device.

H 16. What is a transistor? Name the three terminals which are found on a transistor. Show by a labelled diagram how you would connect a transistor to a battery. Give two practical uses of a transistor.

H 17. What is a transducer? Name a transducer that will convert:
   (a) sound to electricity
   (b) temperature to electricity
   (c) light to electricity.

H 18. Draw a circuit (i) for a burglar alarm which is activated when a burglar shines a light on a photocell (ii) for a fire alarm which is activated when a thermistor is heated.

Energy Conversions

Key Points

1. The **primary source of energy** available to us comes from the **sun**.

2. **Potential energy** is **stored energy**. Examples: fossil fuels, nuclear energy, a coiled spring.

3. **Kinetic energy** is **energy due to movement**. It is dependent on the mass and speed of the object. Examples: a plane flying, a car driving along a road.

4. Energy can be converted from one form to another. Examples:
   (a) mechanical energy to sound energy: a percussion instrument
   (b) potential energy to heat energy: burning coal or oil
   (c) chemical energy to electrical energy to light and heat: a torch
   (d) light energy to electric energy to kinetic energy: a light meter in a camera.

5. **Food** contains **potential energy** (stored energy) which is released in the body by the process of **respiration**.

6. An **electromagnet** is made when current flows through an electric wire which is coiled around a soft iron core. Electromagnets are used in scrap yards for moving scrap metal and in electric bells.

7. When a current carrying wire is placed in a magnetic field, it experiences a force. An application of this is the **electric motor**.

H 8. The **dynamo effect** occurs when a conductor is moved through a magnetic field resulting in the production of a current.

H 9. A **transformer** is a device for increasing or decreasing A.C. voltage. A **step up transformer** increases the voltage and a **step down transformer** decreases the voltage.

$$\frac{V_p}{N_p} = \frac{V_s}{N_s}$$

where V_p = voltage in the primary coil
   V_s = voltage in the secondary coil
   N_p = Number of turns in the primary coil
   N_s = Number of turns in the secondary coil.

Questions

1. What is the primary source of energy available to man?

2. Define
   (a)   potential energy   (b)   kinetic energy.
   Give two examples in each case.

H 3. On what two factors does the kinetic energy of a body depend?

4. Give an example of the following energy conversions in practice:
   (a)   mechanical energy to heat energy
   (b)   mechanical energy to sound energy
   (c)   chemical energy to electric energy to heat energy
   (d)   electric energy to kinetic energy
   (e)   light energy to electric energy to heat and light
   (f)   chemical energy to kinetic energy
   (g)   kinetic energy to electric energy to light energy.

5. List as many energy changes that you can think of which take place in the following (there may be more than one):
   (a)   a washing machine   (b)   an electric food mixer
   (c)   a car   (d)   a dog
   (e)   a television   (f)   a light meter
   (g)   a telephone   (h)   a torch
   (i)   a microphone   (j)   a Crook's radiometer.

6. Describe how you would demonstrate in the laboratory the release of energy from food. Illustrate your answer with a diagram.
   Explain how the energy in a typical breakfast came from the sun.

7. What is an electromagnet?
   How does an electromagnet differ from a permanent magnet?
   Outline an experiment to construct an electromagnet.
   Can an electromagnet be constructed using A.C. current?
   How would you increase the strength of an electromagnet?
   Give three practical uses of an electromagnet in everyday life.

H 8. Name the parts of the electric bell A, B, C, D, E, F, G.
Fig. 4.17
Using the diagram, describe how an electric bell operates.

9. Describe how you would demonstrate that a current carrying wire in a magnetic field experiences a force. Name a device which uses this principle.

10. Label the parts of the electric motor shown in the diagram *Fig. 4.18*.
Briefly outline how the electric motor in the diagram operates.
List three energy conversions which take place in the electric motor.
Name four appliances in the home which make use of an electric motor.

H 11. Sketch the apparatus you would use to produce a voltage by the movement of a magnet through a conductor.
What is this device called? Where would you find such a device? What energy conversions take place in such a device?

12. What is a transformer?
What feature of a transformer determines if it is:
(i) a step-up transformer
(ii) a step-down transformer?
Does a transformer operate with A.C. or D.C. current?
Identify the types of transformers illustrated in the diagram.
Identify the parts A, B and C in *Fig. 4.19*

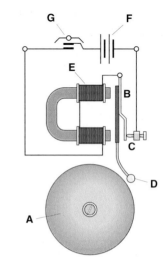

Fig. 4.17

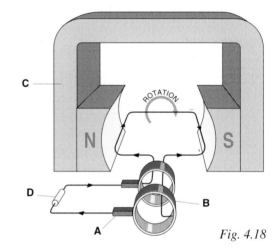

Fig. 4.18

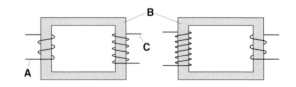

Fig. 4.19

H 13. Write down the formula which relates: the input voltage, the output voltage, the number of turns in the primary coil and the number of turns in the secondary coil.

Give two examples in each case where:

(a) a step-up transformer

(b) a step-down transformer are used.

Fill in the missing figures:

	voltage (primary)	voltage (secondary)	number of turns (primary)	number of turns (secondary)
transformer 1	240	12	1000	?
transformer 2	24	480	?	100
transformer 3	50	?	1500	3000
transformer 4	?	40	50	200

NOTES

NOTES

NOTES

50p OFF

Dear customer, you may use this voucher to save 50p off your next purchase of any title from the Revision Handbook Series.

A limit of one voucher per book applies.

To the retailer: The Educational Company promises to redeem this voucher at face value, provided it has been accepted as part-payment for a second or subsequent purchase from the Revision Handbook Series.

50p off your next purchase